THE LEGAL SYSTEM OF FRANCE

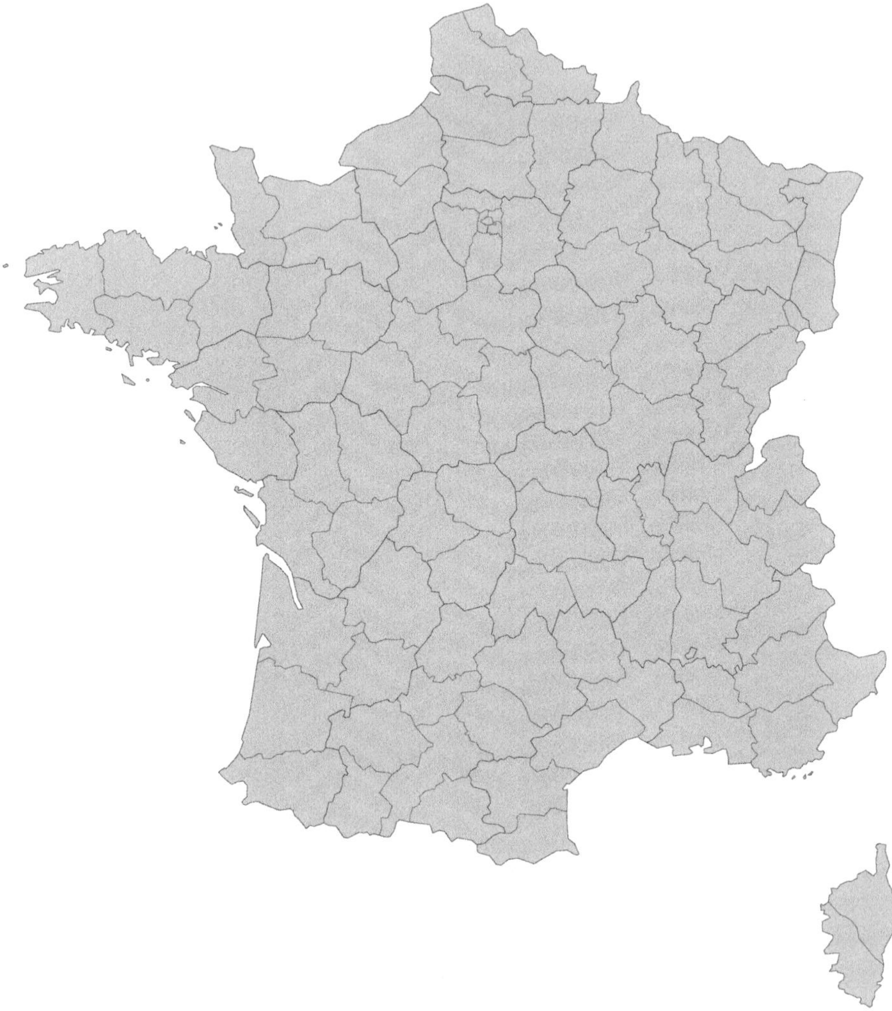

Bibliothèque de l'Association
Henri Capitant

*Library of the Association
Henri Capitant*

LEGAL SYSTEMS SERIES

THE LEGAL SYSTEM OF FRANCE

EDITORS

Alain A. Levasseur
Professor of Law Emeritus, LSU

J. Randall Trahan
Professor of Law, LSU

David Gruning
Professor of Law, Loyola New Orleans

Carolina Academic Press
Durham, North Carolina

Association
Henri Capitant

LGDJ une marque de Lextenso

ISBN: 978-1-5310-1452-0
eISBN: 978-1-5310-1453-7
LCCN: 2019949693

Carolina Academic Press
700 Kent Street
Durham, North Carolina 27701
Telephone (919) 489-7486
Fax (919) 493-5668
www.cap-press.com

Printed in the United States of America

THE SERIES

The Association Henri Capitant has been working to disseminate, modernise and promote civil law for over eight decades. It has traditionally focused on national and international days and bilateral symposia or seminars, which it organises on a regular basis.

As part of the Association's tireless efforts in pursuit of its objectives, its Deputy General Secretary, Cyril Grimaldi, came up with the idea of creating the "Association Henri Capitant Library". The Association's national groups were therefore invited to explain the broad outlines of their law in a series of books, all based on an identical structure, with a limited character count, to give readers the chance to explore and compare the foundations and fundamental features of various systems of law.

As a result, each book in the collection features chapters on the history of the law, its sources, the constitutional framework, legal professionals, criminal law, legal persons, family, property, contracts, liability, quasi-contracts, businesses and labour law.

This provides an invaluable introduction to each system of law, and more besides. Any member of the Association with a user name (visit http://www.henricapitant.org to register) can contact the authors of any of the books by e-mail to discuss issues with them (bibliothequecapitant@lextenso.fr).

The new collection is clearly of immense value, giving everyone the opportunity to explore and understand the substance and spirit that make up and inspire the various systems of foreign law featured in the series. Its contribution to comparative law is simply unparalleled; it offers undoubted benefits to all those who understand the value of stepping outside the boundaries of their own law to better appreciate it and draw inspiration from other forms of law to support its development.

Denis Mazeaud
Professeur, Université Panthéon-Assas (Paris II)

Philippe Dupichot
Professeur, Université Panthéon-Sorbonne (Paris I)

Cyril Grimaldi
Professeur, Université Paris XIII

Alain Levasseur
Professor, LSU Law School

Randall Trahan
Professor, LSU Law School

David Gruning
Professor, Loyola Law School

CHAPTER AUTHORS

Laurent Aynès
Professor of Law,
University of Paris I, Sorbonne
Contract

Martine Béhar-Touchais
Professor of Law,
University of Paris I, Sorbonne
Business Entities

Camille Broyelle
Professor of Law,
University of Paris II, Panthéon-Assas
Constitutional Framework

Rémy Cabrillac
Professor of Law,
University of Montpellier, School of Law and Political Science
Sources of Law

Jean-Paul Decorps
Notary
Legal Actors

Jean-Claude Dubarry
Honorary counsel, Paris Bar
Legal Actors

Philippe Dupichot
Professor of Law,
University of Paris I, Sorbonne
Business Entities

Cyril Grimaldi
Professor of Law,
University of Paris 13
Quasi-Contracts

Michel Grimaldi
Professor of Law,
University of Paris II, Panthéon-Assas
The Family

Hélène Hoepffner
Professor of Law,
University of Toulouse I
Contract

Camille Jauffret-Spinosi
Professor of Law Emeritus,
University of Paris II
Legal History

Francis Kessler
Lecturer in Law,
University of Paris I, Sorbonne
Barrister, Senior counsel, Gide Loyrette Nouel, Paris
Labor and Employment Law

François-Xavier Lucas
Professor of Law, University of Paris I, Sorbonne
Business Entities

Patrick Maistre du Chambon
Professor of Law,
University of Grenoble
Criminal Law

Astrid Marais
Professor of Law,
University of Western Brittany
Persons

François-Xavier Matteoli
Attorney, CMS Bureau Francis Lefebvre
Criminal law

Denis Mazeaud
Professor of Law,
University of Paris II, Panthéon-Assas
Delictual Liability

Laurent Pfister
Professor of Law,
University of Paris II, Panthéon-Assas
Legal History

Foulques de Rostolan
Attorney, Gide Loyrette Nouel, Paris
Labor and Employment law

Philippe Simler
Professor of Law Emeritus, University of Strasbourg,
Honorary Dean, Law School, Political Science
and Management
Property

TABLE OF CONTENTS

THE LEGAL SYSTEM OF FRANCE

CHAPTER ONE

LEGAL HISTORY

French law has its roots in Roman law and it is on this basis that it belongs to the family of Roman or civil law systems.

Roman legal advisers, in spite of using a mainly casuistical method, were the first to propose a theoretical approach to the law, characterised by efforts to establish definitions and draw distinctions, for example between private and public law, or for contracts, crimes, etc. The Romans also produced a coherent set of rules, which were highly valuable in technical terms. Some dealt with the presumption of paternity, servitudes or more generally, the law of obligations. Roman law was equally elaborate in criminal matters. Rome was familiar with both adversarial proceedings involving a jury, and investigative proceedings guided by the judge's firm conviction and subject to the presumption of innocence. Finally, public law was not uninfluential on the development of modern states.

Roman law survived the disappearance of Roman civilisation thanks to the Christian church and the compilations of law ordered by Justinian, the Eastern Roman emperor, in the 6th century, which were rediscovered in Italy in the 12th century.

The fall of the Western Roman empire, in 476, led to a period of pluralism in legal sources and rules. Despite the formation of a unified state, this pluralism persisted until the French Revolution. Nonetheless, it has evolved over these 13 centuries and paved the way for the development of a "French law" in the modern era.

In the early Middle Ages, the various ethnic groups that lived under the authority of the Frankish kings each retained their own law. Two legal traditions co-existed under this system, which was based on the principle of the personality of laws: Roman law, which applied to the Gallo-Romans but was gradually disappearing, and Germanic customs, under the form of laws such as the Salic Law (507). At the same time, the Church, which was connected to the Merovingians by the baptism of Clovis (496) and the Carolingians through coronation, strove to impose its own rules—canon law—on the whole of society. The status of slaves improved, becoming closer to that of half-slaves and gradually resulting in serfdom. Grants of land, linked to personal relationships, were very common and heralded the start of the feudal/vassal system. Contractual and marital relationships were formalised, with the Church attempting—not without some difficulty—to add a moral element to the latter. Family solidarity came to the fore in criminal matters, with the authorities struggling to eradicate acts of private vengeance, or in inheritance issues, the desire to keep property in the family providing grounds for the exclusion of women.

Legal pluralism based on ethnic groups became a territorial issue during the 10th and 11th centuries.

Territorial customs became increasingly fragmented and were replaced by the feudal system. The Capetian kingdom was not only a mosaic of seigneuries but also, in both northern and southern France, a mosaic of customs that were valid in different jurisdictions. Customs were crystallised through disputes. Some of them were written down, as official texts in the south of France and private compilations in the north, such as Beaumanoir's: *The Coutumes de Beauvaisis* (1283). Customs governed numerous areas of private law. The unequal status of people, noblemen and members of the Third Estate is one example. They also governed areas such as matrimonial property and inheritance, based on principles of community, lineage and inequality. Feudalism was subject to the influence of customs, which also extended to public law. The repetition of customs resulted in several rules on succession to the

Crown, which, along with others, would form the fundamental laws of the kingdom, later known as the "customary constitution".

Two other sources supplemented or influenced customs: canon law and Roman law, considered as universal learned law because they were taught in Latin, in universities throughout Europe from the 12th century onwards.

Canon law reached its peak in the second half of the Middle Ages. Gradually compiled in the *Corpus iuris canonici*, pontifical law was applied and sometimes enhanced by the ecclesiastical courts, as well as discussed by an abundance of creative legal thinkers. The Church strove to impose Christian discipline on a secular society, particularly in matrimonial matters: formed by the consent of the couple only, the sacrament of marriage was deemed indissoluble, although separation and division of property were accepted. By extension, filiation was also governed by canon law.

The renaissance of Roman law in the 12th century, linked to the rise of ecclesiastical law, is a critical event in the history of law in general. Justinian's rediscovered compilations, the *Corpus iuris civilis*, were studied first in Bologna and then in most universities in Europe. This was the rebirth of a real science of law, illustrated by the work of both glossators and, later, commentators. Roman law was viewed, alongside canon law, as the *jus commune*, a general common law that was deemed superior to local laws and destined to supplant them. Its penetration was driven by notaries, lawyers and judges. The dotal system (the right and power of a husband to administer his wife's dotal property) and wills reemerged, particularly in the south of France. The Roman law of contract, enhanced by consensualism, became universally established. Legal proceedings were based on a model that combined elements of Roman and canon law. Justinian's compilations were also relied upon by the Kings of France in building and shaping a sovereign, independent state.

Political independence, which had been achieved at the end of the Middle Ages, was now combined with legal independence. The idea of a "French law" or "common law of France" was developed in response to canon and Roman law, which were viewed as foreign. Formulated by legal thinkers in the 16th century, the idea was ratified by a royal edict of 1679, which created the teaching of "French law". Nonetheless, legal pluralism did not completely disappear in the modern era; it did, however, change.

Canon law lost some of its influence, notably because the king, as lawmaker, and his parliaments began to interfere in matters that had previously fallen within the sole jurisdiction of the Church. Roman law was widely accepted in the south of France, but on the basis of a custom that was tolerated by the king. Its acceptance there resulted in a separation between the regions to the south of a line between the Ile d'Oléron and Lake Geneva, which were governed by written law, and the customary law in the north of the country.

In these northern regions, Roman law played a purely auxiliary role as written reason, with no binding force. Nonetheless, its influence was significant, in particular in the law of obligations. It was also associated with the expression of natural law, particularly by Jean Domat whose book *Les lois civiles dans leur ordre naturel* (1689) would, in part, inspire the writers of the Civil Code.

In the strict sense of the term, "French law" consisted of customs and laws made by the king. The consequence of the official written versions, ordered in 1453, and their later revisions, was to protect the customs of the north from a massive influx of Roman law, reduce their number and deal with discrepancies. Legal thinking contributed to this process by identifying a "customary common law", often based on the customs of Paris. Another source of French law, law from by the king, glorified by the supporters of an absolute monarchy, became increasingly dominant in private law. During the 16th century, orders were issued, establishing French as the language of the law, and setting out the rules on marriage. Codification orders were promulgated during the reign of Louis XIV, notably in relation to civil and criminal procedure, in 1667 and 1670 respectively. In the 18th century, significant orders were issued concerning gifts, wills and substitution, prepared by the chancellor D'Aguesseau.

Like others before him, D'Aguesseau had envisaged a unification of the law. But in reality, at the end of the Ancien Régime, "French law was not a single, uniform law throughout the kingdom, but a combination" of various sources (Diderot and d'Alembert, *Encyclopédie*). Pothier († 1772), a professor of French law in Orléans, offered a comprehensive account of this "combination", which would later inspire the drafters of the Civil Code. The fact remained that on the basis of reason and equality, the pluralism of the old law was criticised and unification became the order of the day.

The French Revolution was the first step towards it. The leaders of the revolution wanted to unify law to express new ideas in rules that would be applicable to all French people, without exception. The Constitution of 1791 provided for the creation of a French Civil Code. Three drafts were produced under Cambacérès' leadership, but it was not until Napoléon came to power that French private law was unified.

The decision to draft the Civil Code was made at Napoléon's instigation. As Jean-Louis Halperin points out, Napoléon intended to "complete the Revolution by preserving its principal achievements, strengthening and organising the social fabric, and increasing the power of the State through greater uniformity and centralisation". A drafting committee was appointed on 12 August 1800. Napoleon selected the four members: Tronchet, Maleville, Bigot de Préameneu and Portalis. The work would take them just five months, with a draft code produced by 21 January 1801. It was submitted to the courts for comment, then to the Conseil d'Etat (in which Napoleon often participated) for discussion and finally, to the assemblies. It was promulgated as the *French Civil Code* on March 21, 1804.

The personality and background of the four members of the committee influenced both the drafting and content of the Code. All four practiced law, had trained under the Ancien Régime, were broadly moderate in outlook, and were familiar with both the strengths of the Revolution and the mistakes made. Their aim was to give French citizens a new system of law, inspired by the law of the Ancien Régime, since the intention was not to completely overturn the landscape of French law, but carefully introduce the new ideas of equality and freedom developed by the Enlightenment philosophers and supporters of natural law.

The law of the Ancien Régime gave the drafters of the Code the law of obligations, which was broadly inherited from Roman law. In other areas, such as matrimonial regimes, they chose from the various existing customs. But they also innovated. With regard to ownership of immovable property, for example, their aim was to prevent any return of a feudal system. Inheritance law was profoundly altered to establish equality between heirs. The secularisation of marriage and acceptance of divorce established by the Revolution were confirmed in the Code.

The Civil Code established the supremacy of statutory law as the primary source of law. However, the Code and its drafters also recognised the role of judges, despite the reluctance of the revolutionaries.

The Code only governed the relationship between private individuals. Public law and, in particular, relations between the administrative authorities and individuals were not codified.

A constitution, preceded by a Declaration of Rights, was intended to underpin the new political system the revolutionaries wanted. Three constitutions were drafted, in 1791, 1793 and 1795, inspired by the ideas of the philosophers of the Enlightenment era. These established the sovereignty of the nation and the principle of the separation of powers. The Declaration of the Rights of Man and of the Citizen that preceded the Constitution of 1791 is still referenced in the French Constitution of 1958.

The Civil Code was praised throughout the 19th century. Legal writers analysed it in detail, commending its style and the ideas it contained. Its genuine qualities inspired a large number of foreign lawmakers, who were keen to have a code that answered new aspirations.

Case law has played a very significant role in the long-term survival of the Civil Code. Portalis had emphasised that codes are time-bound and cannot govern everything. It has fallen to the judiciary to interpret the Code as times have changed, creating a body of case law in the 19th and especially in the 20th centuries, which has allowed the Code to remain in effect. Examples include the area of liability, the very broad interpretation of article 1382 and the creation of liability for things under one's custody.

Case law has also played a decisive role in administrative law. This branch of law is a judicial creation and like *common law*, it was formed casuistically, with the Conseil d'Etat carefully overseeing its development in various areas: public property, contracts with the administration, the liability of public authorities, etc.

In spite of the judges' efforts, time began to reveal weaknesses or inadequacies in the Civil Code from the 20th century onwards. Some legal thinkers had been critical and had called for the revision of the Code. These attempts did not, however, proved successful. Nonetheless, some areas have been fundamentally changed and new rules have been inserted into the Code. In the 1970s, for example, Doyen Carbonier reformulated whole swathes of family law. Recently, the law on suretyship has been amended and changes to the law of contract are currently being planned (see the reforms of 2016–2017). But alongside these successful efforts to keep the Code alive, a large number of special statutes have been adopted, the content of which has remained outside the Code, such as the 1965 act on joint ownership or the Badinter Act of 1985, improving the status of victims of traffic accidents. It is also important to remember the new "codes" that bring together the rules in a particular area, such as the Labor Code or Consumer Code.

French law today no longer consists solely of rules from French institutions: the rapidly increasing number of rules derived from international and supranational law must be applied by French judges, even if they are contrary to French legislative provisions or case law. European Union directives, regulations and conventions thus apply either directly or indirectly, along with the decisions of the European Court of Justice, the rulings of the European Court of Human Rights in Strasbourg, and the rules laid down in the international conventions ratified by France, such as the 1980 Vienna Convention on the International Sale of Goods. All of these regulations, which must be applied by French judges, have led to a kind of judicialisation of French law, with case law playing an equal or even superior role to legislation.

However, it is important to emphasise that the internationalisation of law, which tends, to some extent, to unify national rights, is not without its detractors. The reaction is a form of legal nationalism. States often defend their own law and create new codes to do so. In France, this form of nationalism was manifested by the creation of the "priority question on constitutionality" in 2010. This procedure is a means of limiting the intervention of "foreign" judges, particularly from the court in Strasbourg, in assessing French law. This clearly reflects a desire to ensure the primacy of French law over international or supranational law.

CHAPTER TWO

SOURCES OF LAW

French law is still marked by the hierarchy of norms systematised by Kelsen, the usefulness of which is decisive insofar as a lower norm can neither depart from, nor repeal, a higher norm.

All written sources of French law can be found on the Legifrance website (www.legifrance.gouv.fr).

The Constitution of 4 October 1958 sits at the top of the hierarchy of norms. In a famous decision of 16 July 1971, the Constitutional Council included in it the preamble to the Constitution and the texts to which it refers, the Declaration of the Rights of Man of 1789 and the Preamble of the 1946 Constitution. Together, these norms form what legal writers call the "bloc de constitutionalité" or corpus of constitutional rules. A Constitutional Act of 29 May 2005, supplementing the first paragraph of the Preamble of the Constitution, added the Environmental Charter of 2004.

The pre-eminence of the Constitution over international treaties is based on its article 54, which makes ratification or approval of an international undertaking that is contrary to the Constitution dependent on amending it. The Constitution's pre-eminence has been challenged by European law (ECJ, 15 July 1964, *Costa*), but the Cour de Cassation has consistently upheld it (Plenary session, 2 June 2000).

International treaties rank second in the hierarchy, provided that they are lawfully ratified and applied by the other party (article 55 of the Constitution). Among the various international treaties, separate treatment is reserved for the European Convention on Human Rights, which was adopted by the Council of Europe on 4 November 1950 and ratified by France on 3 May 1974 (see the Council of Europe portal: www.coe.int). The text has been supplemented by several additional protocols, which have added further rights and freedoms to those covered by the Convention or modified the monitoring system. The importance of the European Convention on Human Rights is justified by the area of law it covers, which means it is referred to increasingly frequently in national courts. Above all, it derives from the institutional mechanism that underpins it. A case can be referred to the European Court of Human Rights (ECHR) established by the Convention, and which sits in Strasbourg, by an individual person once she has exhausted her national rights of appeal (to read the rulings of the ECHR, see: www.echr.coe.int). While a ruling by the ECHR acknowledging a breach of the Convention by a state does not, in principle, offer the claimant the possibility of their case being re-examined by a national court (apart from in exceptional criminal cases), it generally does give rise to a change in the national legislation or jurisprudence, to make one or the other compliant with the Convention.

European Union law (see the European Union portal: www.europa.net), derived from the three founding treaties (the Treaty of Paris of 25 July 1952 and the Treaties of Rome of 25 March 1957) and several later treaties (the most recent being the Lisbon Treaty of 13 December 2007), supplemented by secondary legislation, consisting in regulations (which are general in scope, fully binding and directly applicable in each Member State), directives (which are binding on all States in terms of the result they need to achieve, but which leave the means by which it is achieved to the discretion of the state concerned) and decisions (all elements of which are obligatory), plays a fundamental role in French law, as it does in other EU Member States. The Court of Justice of the European Union (CJEU, previously the Court of Justice of the European Communities—CJEC), which sits in Luxembourg, ensures the uniformity of the interpretation of European law, through the preliminary ruling on interpretation; if a difficulty of interpretation arises, national courts can and—if it is a court whose rulings allow no possibility of an appeal—must stay the proceedings and refer the question of interpretation to the Court (to access the decisions of the Court of Justice, see: www.curia.europa.eu).

The next level down in the hierarchy of sources of law is occupied by legislation and regulations, which exist alongside each other. This co-existence is the result of a genuine legal revolution produced by the 1958 Constitution. Statutory law is limited in scope to the matters listed in article 34 of the Constitution: statutes lay down the rules for some matters (for example: the civil rights and fundamental guarantees granted to citizens for the exercise of civil liberties, nationality, the status and capacity of individuals, etc.) and the fundamental principles of other matters (for example: the system of property ownership, rights in rem and civil obligations). Conversely, regulations have the right to establish principles (article 37 of the Constitution).

Are included at this level of the hierarchy:

- statutes, legislation;
- referendum adopted in accordance with article 11 of the Constitution, following a referendum held according to the conditions set out in the same article;
- decisions taken by the President of the Republic pursuant to article 16 of the Constitution, which grants him or her exceptional powers in a period of serious crisis;
- orders issued pursuant to article 38 of the Constitution, which allows the Government to ask Parliament the authority to take measures, for a limited period, in areas that would normally fall under statute law;
- regulations enacted in accordance with article 37 of the Constitution, which are called executive regulations.

At the next lower level are the so-called implementing regulations for statutes, in the areas reserved for statutes by article 34 of the Constitution.

It should be noted that ministerial circulars (administrative documents produced by a ministry for their staff, to guide them in applying a piece of legislation or regulation), are not binding.

France, the homeland of codification, has compiled a large proportion of its regulatory and legislative provisions in some 60 codes. The most emblematic one dates back to the Napoleonic codifications and they have been gradually (e.g. the : Civil Code) or completely (e.g. the : Criminal Code) updated. Most codes are written without changing the existing law.

The Constitutional Council checks the compliance of international treaties with the Constitution on the basis of article 54 (to access the decisions of the Constitutional Council, see: www.conseil-constitutionnel.fr). This procedure was resorted to on several occasions in recent years, in relation to adopting European Union treaties. For example, a revision of the Constitution on 4 February 2008 preceded France's ratification of the Lisbon Treaty on 14 February 2008.

According to article 61 of the Constitution, a statute can be referred to the Constitutional Council prior to its promulgation, to verify its compliance with the Constitution. A statute that is declared unconstitutional cannot be promulgated. Conversely, once a statute has been declared to be in compliance with the Constitution, its constitutionality cannot be challenged by the courts: the decisions of the Constitutional Council are binding on the public authorities, and on all administrative and judicial authorities.

A revision of the constitution on 23 July 2008 introduced the "priority question on constitutionality" (QPC). This is a mechanism that allows citizens to challenge a statute that has already come into effect before an administrative or ordinary court, if it is deemed contrary to the rights and freedoms guaranteed by the Constitution. The administrative and ordinary courts act as a filter, since in order to be admissible and referred to the Constitutional

Council, a question must be new or serious in nature. A statute that is declared unconstitutional will be repealed as soon as the Constitutional Council's decision is published, or on the date set in the decision.

Nonetheless, it is important to state that certain laws are not subject to a review of constitutionality: they are referendum statutes and decisions taken by the President of the Republic pursuant to article 16 of the Constitution. Finally, the Constitutional Council has ruled that it is not competent to assess the compliance with the Constitution of a law that is confined to drawing the necessary consequences of a directive. The Council reserved only the right to censure a law that transposes a directive into national law when it conflicts with a rule or principle inherent to France's constitutional identity.

Laws must also comply with international treaties. While it is unanimously agreed that a treaty implicitly repeals a prior law that contradicted it, the issue has raised difficulties with subsequent laws.

In a decision dated 15 January 1975, the Constitutional Council ruled that it was not competent to assess the compliance of a law with an international treaty. The issue resulted in a famous disagreement between the Cour de Cassation and the Conseil d'Etat. The former quickly decided that a treaty should prevail over a subsequent contradicting law (Joint bench, 24 May 1975). For a long time, the Conseil d'Etat (Council of State) rejected this position (CE, 1 March 1968, *Syndicat général des fabricants de semoule de France*) but later reversed its jurisprudence (CE, 20 October 1989, *Nicolo*).

Executive regulations are not governed by statute but are nonetheless subject to review by the Conseil d'Etat, in charge of verifying their compliance with the corpus of constitutional rules.

A review of the legality of the implementing regulations of particular statutes can be carried out by the administrative and ordinary courts. The review can take the form of an application to annul the regulation on grounds of abuse of authority; it can only be referred to the administrative courts, as the nullity has effect *erga omnes*. However, the legality of a regulation can also be contested by means of a plea of illegality, which allows a regulation that has been declared illegal to be ignored in relation to a particular dispute. A plea of illegality can be freely submitted to the administrative courts. Since the ordinary courts cannot encroach on the prerogatives of the executive, a plea of illegality is admissible in the criminal courts but is admissible in the civil courts only if the disputed regulation infringes one's individual freedom or the right of ownership.

As regards unwritten sources, a distinction is made between *case law*, custom, general principles and doctrine, the writings of jurists.

In the period immediately following the Revolution, French law—influenced by Enlightenment philosophy and the theory of separation of powers—considered that the judge was "no more than the mouth that pronounces the words of the law", according to Montesquieu's famous expression. Article 5 of the Civil Code thus prohibits decisions that set a precedent: a court cannot adopt a general solution that would apply to all similar disputes that may be referred to it in the future. Prohibiting rulings that set a precedent is a continuation of the principle of the relative authority of res judicata (Civ. Code, art. 1355): a court decision only binds the two parties involved in the dispute. These principles mean that precedents have no binding force: a decision made by a court of any kind does not bind other courts that are subsequently called to rule in a similar case.

However, a judge may find that the law is silent or contradictory on the issue concerned. Article 4 of the Civil Code prohibits a denial of justice: any litigant has the right to have his claim heard and adjuged by a court. Accordingly, the Cour de Cassation has issued decisions amounting to principles that carry significant moral, if not legal authority. For example: the general principle of liability for things that someone has under his/her custody, abuse of rights, unjust enrichment, the general principle of liability for the actions of others, estoppel, etc. Decisions of this nature create precedents and the solution they offer is adopted, often expressed in precisely the same terms, by courts hearing and judging a similar case (to access the rulings of the Cour de Cassation, see: www.courdecassation.fr).

Custom, which is multiform, plays only a residual role.

Custom can be recognised as having a role by the law itself (custom *secundum legem*). For example, article 1194 of the Civil Code refers to "usage" to determine the extent of the obligations of the parties. The law may also refer to custom through certain notions such as good morals ("bonnes moeurs") (e.g. : Civil Code art. 6).

Custom may develop in the absence of law (custom *praeter legem*). Business practices, for example, are playing an increasing role in labor relations. This is also the case in business relationships, particularly in international trade law.

However, custom cannot prevail over legislation (custom *contra legem*). Even prolonged tolerance of a practice that is *contra legem* does not mean the law is repealed.

The *general principles* set out in a legislative, regulatory or other text have the authority of the law or regulation of which they form a part.

The general principles identified by the courts have their own authority, their position in the hierarchy of norms varying: certain principles are of constitutional authority and bind the legislature, while others only have the authority of a statute.

Legal writings or doctrine cannot be considered a source of law, if only because the opinions of legal writers are often different or even conflicting.

Nonetheless, doctrine is an indirect source of law because of its authority. Doctrince has a significant influence on both statute law and case law.

CHAPTER THREE

THE CONSTITUTIONAL FRAMEWORK

France's constitutional framework is formed by the Constitution of 4 October 1958.

1. CONSTITUTION

1.1. MAIN CHARACTERISTICS OF THE CONSTITUTION

The Constitution of the 5th Republic establishes a hybrid political system. It combines the characteristics of a parliamentary system (under which the government is accountable to Parliament, which the President of the Republic has the power to dissolve) and those of a presidential system in which the President is directly elected by universal suffrage and has a far more influential role than the Prime Minister, particularly since the President's term of office—five years—has been aligned with that of members of the National Assembly. The hybrid system established by the 1958 Constitution is sometimes described as "semi-presidential".

The Constitution sets out the fundamental rights which are, in most cases, laid down in the texts to which its Preamble refers. The first is the Declaration of the Rights of Man of 1789, which establishes the fundamental freedoms the State cannot challenge (rights of ownership, freedom of thought and opinion, and freedom of association). These are classified as "first-generation" rights. Next, the text of the 1946 Preamble, which sets out a list of economic and social rights (the right to work, health and education, as well as the right to strike) referred to as "second-generation" rights. Finally, the Environmental Charter, which sets out rights and obligations in respect of the environment (such as the right to participate in decisions with an impact on the environment, the duty to repair damage caused to the environment and the precautionary principle), classified as "third-generation" rights.

Together, these texts form the "bloc de constitutionnalité" or corpus of constitutional rules; the legislature's compliance with these rules is sanctioned by specific procedures of control, brought before the Constitutional Council (Conseil Constitutionnel). These consist, first, in an *a priori* review, provided for in the 1958 Constitution: as the name implies, this review is carried out before the law is promulgated, and it is open to specific political authorities (the President of the Republic, the Prime Minister, the presidents of the National Assembly and the Senate, 60 members of the National Assembly or 60 senators). A law that is not in compliance is censured and does not come into force. Next, an *a posteriori* review, which was introduced by the revision of the Constitution of 23 July 2008. This offers to potential litigants the opportunity to challenge a law that infringes the "rights and freedoms" guaranteed by the Constitution. The challenge (or "ground") is formulated as a "priority question on constitutionality" (QPC) submitted to the Constitutional Council by the Conseil d'Etat (Council of State) or the Cour de Cassation, depending on which court is involved. If the Constitutional Council rules that the ground is justified (i.e. the law infringes a right or freedom guaranteed by the Constitution), the law is repealed.

The 1958 Constitution can be classified as a "rigid" constitution: amending it is subject to particular procedures, different from those that apply to the adoption of an ordinary law. Two procedures may be followed. One is referred to in article 89 of the Constitution: once the change to the Constitution has been adopted in identical terms by both houses (the National Assembly and the Senate), it is adopted by a referendum or in Congress (i.e. a meeting of both houses), by a three-fifths majority of the votes cast. The other option, which the authors of the Constitution did not envisage as a means of revising it, is the procedure defined in article 11, which allows any bill relating to the "organisation of the public authorities" to be submitted to a direct referendum. This procedure—which allows the executive to dispense with the agreement of Parliament—was used by General de Gaulle to change the method of electing the President of the Republic (through the introduction of direct universal suffrage). This method of revising the Constitution, which some describe as "constitutional custom", was used on one other occasion, this time unsuccessfully (in 1969, for a change involving the Senate) and has fallen into disuse. Twenty-three of the 24 amendments to the 1958 Constitution have been adopted according to the procedure set out in article 89.

1.2. STRUCTURE OF THE STATE

The 1958 Constitution establishes a unitary, decentralised state.

Unitary, because of the dominant principle of indivisibility ("France shall be an indivisible [...] Republic", art. 1), as a result of which, in particular, only the State holds legislative power. The unity of the State is also manifested by the existence of administrative and financial controls exercised by the State over the public authorities established in it. Its "decentralised organisation", as enshrined in article 1 of the Constitution, is expressed in tangible terms by the existence of local authorities (communes, departments and regions) with their own powers, which are "self-governing through elected councils" (art. 72). More specifically, local authorities "may take decisions in all matters arising under powers that can best be exercised at their level" (art. 72), on the understanding that the legislature decides which level of authority is competent, under the (limited) control of the Constitutional Council. In order to carry out their role, local authorities have a degree of financial independence ("revenue of which they may dispose freely", art. 72-2) and have the power to make regulations (art. 72). They also have been allowed to depart from statutory law since the constitutional reform of 28 March 2003. However, their involvement in the legislative domain is strictly limited: it must be authorised by the legislature, it must state the reason for its action and it may only be on an experimental basis, for a limited period, after which the legislature will have the option either to extend the rule to all local authorities of the same level, or repeal it.

Special mention should be made of the overseas departments and regions, governed by articles 73 and 74 of the Constitution, that have more autonomy than the other local authorities, and New Caledonia (title XIII of the Constitution), which is almost a federated entity.

2. CONSTITUTIONAL POWERS

2.1. LEGISLATIVE POWER

The Constitution establishes an asymmetric bicameral system. The National Assembly—or "lower house"—is made up of 577 members, elected by direct universal suffrage, on the basis of a single majority vote in two ballots, for a five-year term. The Senate –made up of 348 senators elected by indirect universal suffrage for six years—is the "upper chamber". It represents the "territorial communities" (art. 24).

The National Assembly and the Senate vote on legislation in the domains defined by the Constitution (art. 34: civil liberties, the status of individuals, crimes and other serious offences, tax and property ownership). Both houses have the power to initiate legislation, along with the government. However, their role is residual: laws proposed by the National Assembly or the Senate can neither reduce income nor increase expenditure and the government has priority on the order of business of both houses. If there is a disagreement between the two houses, the National Assembly has the final say.

Parliament also exercises control over the government through oral or written questions, or by establishing expert missions or commissions of enquiry. In terms of control, the National Assembly also has more powers than the Senate: only the lower house can overthrow the government.

Finally, the Parliament can adopt resolutions, i.e. opinions (on drafts of European legislation, or any other subject); it ratifies treaties and meets as Congress to revise the Constitution.

2.2. EXECUTIVE POWER

The French Constitution establishes a dual executive power, shared between the President of the Republic, who has the right to dissolve the National Assembly (but is not accountable to it) and the Prime Minister, as head of the government, who is appointed and can be dismissed by the President and is accountable to the Assembly. In practice, the executive power is either effectively held by the President, when their party has a majority in Parliament, or by the Prime Minister if not, during periods of so-called "cohabitation". The government is made up of ministers, led by the Prime Minister, and runs the administration.

The central administration is made up of various departments, each attached to a ministry. These departments carry out their duties under the authority of the minister, who has hierarchical authority, and regulatory power to organise the department. The state's decentralised administration is present throughout the country. The department, under the authority of the 'préfet' is the standard and main decentralised sub-division.

The institutional model of the independent administrative authority has developed since the end of the 1970s. Created by statute (or the Constitution, in the case of the Defender of Rights, for example), as part of the central State and, in principle, without legal personality (apart from some, which are described as "independent public authorities"), they are not subject to any form of state control. It is in that respect that they are independent; however, this does not imply that they are not subject to the control of the courts.

Independent administrative authorities operate in areas in which the traditional administration appears less well suited, precisely because of its involvement with the State: for example, with regard to freedoms (the CNIL for data protection, or the inspector of prisons and other institutions where people are deprived of their liberty), the relationship between the administration and the citizens (the CADA for access to administrative documents) and the field of economic regulation (the AMF, for the regulation of the financial markets, or the ARCEP for economic communications).

2.3. JUDICIAL POWER

The dual structure of the French court system dates back to the law of 16 and 24 August 1790: the judicial power is split between the ordinary courts and the administrative courts.

Each set of courts consists of a hierarchical series of courts, from the courts of first instance up to the appeal courts, with a Supreme Court at the top, which is the Cour de Cassation, for the ordinary courts, and the Conseil d'Etat for the administrative courts. The powers of the two supreme courts are entirely separate because of the historical circumstances that preceded their establishment. The Cour de Cassation that controls the lower courts, has the power to quash an earlier decision. For the Conseil d'Etat, however, this is a relatively recent mission. Until 1953, its role was to judge administrative disputes under the ordinary law; in that year, when the administrative courts were created, it heard cases on appeal under the ordinary law and it was not until 1987, when the administrative appeal courts were created, that quashing earlier decisions became its main role. However, the Conseil d'Etat still judges a significant number of disputes of first and last instance, concerning the actions of the highest state authorities. The Council of State does not act solely as a court; it also has a significant consultative role in assisting the government and gives its opinion on all bills and draft orders.

As a summary, the ordinary general courts can be said to have authority to hear criminal cases and disputes between individuals, and the administrative courts as hearing disputes between private individuals and a public body, or between public bodies. To this summary mainly based on the legal nature of the parties being public or private, can be added a series of criteria (such as whether a public service mission or the prerogatives of public authority are involved), which will determine whether the dispute will be heard in the administrative or the ordinary courts.

Although the legislature may alter here and there the jurisdiction of the courts, a hard core of matters is reserved to each court system by the constitution: administrative decisions can only be overturned by a judge in the administrative courts; the protection of private property and individual freedom (i.e. security) is solely a matter for the ordinary courts.

Difficulties arising in distributing jurisdictional matters between the different orders of courts are decided by the 'Tribunal des Conflits', a court made up of an equal number of members of the Cour de Cassation and of the Conseil d'Etat.

CHAPTER FOUR

LEGAL ACTORS

1. JUDGES ('MAGISTRATS')

Judges are at the heart of the process of applying the law and are vested with the power to ensure the validity of a legal action (such as adopting a child or changing the matrimonial regime applicable to a particular couple) . . . or to settle a dispute. In most cases, they exercise their authority in a state court but may also act in a private setting, for example in arbitration cases.

The role of being a judge is entrusted in the first place to 'magistrats'; they are civil servants who carry out their duties in the lower courts ('tribunaux d'instance' and 'tribunaux de grande instance'), administrative courts, courts of appeal, the Conseil d'Etat and the Cour de Cassation.

Other people also act as judges and there are about four times more of them than there are who work in the administrative or ordinary courts; these are professionals who fulfil the role on a temporary and generally voluntary basis, hearing cases in special courts, such as employment tribunals, commercial courts and agricultural land tribunals; others provide assistance to certain procedures led by professional judges, such as jury members or assessors in the juvenile courts.

The diverse range of functions and statuses is reflected in the recruitment process of these legal actors.

Judges in the ordinary courts are mainly recruited on the basis of competitive examinations; the successful candidates, known as 'auditeurs de justice' are enrolled at the École nationale de la magistrature, where they are trained for 31 months, including numerous work placements and internships.

Alongside the first competitive examination—known as the student competition—which is open to people of French nationality who are not older than 31, there are two others at the same level, one reserved for civil servants or employees of the state or local authorities with four years of service, and the other for people with at least eight years of professional activity. Members of the administrative courts and the Conseil d'Etat are mainly recruited from former students of the Ecole nationale d'administration.

The recruitment of some other judges is an entirely different process. It does not involve a competitive examination but an electoral process.

It applies, for example, to judges of the commercial courts, who must be of French nationality and business owners or corporate directors. They are elected for an initial period of two and then four years, by an electoral college made up of judges or former commercial judges ('juges consulaires') and business representatives ('délégués consulaires') elected by the Chambers of Commerce and Industry.

The electoral process, which had also been in effect for a long time for the appointment of members of employment tribunals from both employers and employees, was recently abandoned because of low turnout in the elections. The law of 11 December 2014 authorised the government to use secondary legislation to decide on a new appointment system, subject to consultations with the trade unions.

Jury members must also be of French nationality and at least 23 years old, and know how to read and write; they are drawn by lot from lists made within the jurisdiction of each cour d'assises (criminal court for serious offences) from initial lists drawn up in the same way in each commune.

2. REGISTRARS ('GREFFIERS')

Registrars are technical experts in procedural matters and assist judges with all sorts of juridical acts. Their role is to ensure the smooth running of the proceedings they attend, draft formal minutes and authenticate decisions, issue copies of them, ensure seals are kept safely, etc.

Registrars in the commercial courts perform the same functions. They also keep and monitor the Register of Trade and Companies, and the public records on immovable transactions.

Staff employed in the registries of the civil and criminal courts and employment tribunals –around 10,000 people—are civil servants who belong to two different groups: registrars, whose duties have been described above, and chief registrars, who are authorised to carry out the same tasks but are primarily involved in management, administration and supervisory roles, participating in the organisation of their court and helping to prepare their budget.

Registrars and chief registrars, of French nationality, are recruited through external competitive examinations which are open to those who hold a baccalaureate plus three years' higher education for chief registrars, or a baccalaureate plus two years for registrars, and internal competitions for those with four years' actual public service. The training lasts for 10 months in all cases and is dispensed at the École nationale des greffiers.

Registrars in the commercial courts—as those in the civil and criminal courts and employment tribunals were previously—are public law officers who are officially appointed by the Ministry of Justice, hold office and are entitled, as are notaries, bailiffs, etc., to present their successor. They must be of French nationality, hold a Master's in law or equivalent qualification, and have passed an aptitude test.

3. BARRISTERS-ATTORNEYS ('AVOCATS')

The oldest and best-known of the barrister-attorney's functions are to provide assistance and representation in court. With the exceptions of the Conseil d'Etat and the civil divisions of the Cour de Cassation, where the relatively small group of special 'avocats aux Conseils' have a monopoly of representation, French attorneys can represent their clients in all civil or administrative courts and other judicial bodies, including disciplinary boards. In criminal cases, where the defendants generally appear in person, they assist their clients during the investigative phase and in the trial court. Even if the defendant does not appear and is not excused, their attorney can still present their defence.

Their activities are not solely confined to the courts, however, and extend to all areas of the law, in the form of opinions, advice and consultations but also drafting contracts and private agreements.

They can also exercise powers that are further removed from their traditional role, for example as a director of a commercial company, fiduciary, data protection officer, agent in immovable property transactions, mandataries-trustees in dealings between a taxpayer and the tax authorities, or even a sports agent!

A barrister or attorney is necessarily a member of a bar; admission is dependent on the candidate being of French nationality and a citizen of the European Union or European Economic Area Member State, or of a bar that grants French citizens the right to practise this professional activity, subject to the same conditions, or have the status of refugee or stateless person as defined by the French Office for the Protection of Refugees and Stateless people (OFPRA). A barrister or lawyer must hold a Master in law or equivalent qualification and the certificate to practise as a barrister (CAPA) issued by the regional professional training centres, after an 18-month course.

Several groups of people are exempt from the requirement to hold either a Master's degree or the CAPA, and often both, namely:

judges and former judges; university professors, former 'avoués', notaries, bailiffs, industrial property advisers and registrars in the commercial courts but also, subject to certain conditions on length of service, some civil servants, corporate lawyers or employees of a barrister or 'avoué'.

Provided these conditions are met, the Bar Council for the bar the candidate is seeking to join will check that there are no obstacles to their admission. The individual concerned then swears an oath before the court of appeal, "to carry out their duties with dignity, conscientiously, independently, honestly and with humanity". They are then entitled to practise independently or for a firm as an employee, self-employed practitioner or partner, and are required to engage in continuing professional development throughout their working life.

The increasing complexity of legislation means that many attorneys have limited their sphere of activity to certain areas. For the last few years, they have been able to state their areas of specialisation, limited to one or two, provided they can submit evidence of an ongoing practice followed by a control.

Attorneys-Barristers at the Conseil d'Etat and the Cour de Cassation, commonly known as "avocats aux Conseils", unlike other 'avocats', are officially appointed pubic officers.

In order to be appointed, either to succeed a colleague who has resigned or as a partner in a firm that holds such an office, the candidate must fulfil the same conditions as regards nationality and qualifications required for other barristers, he must have taken a course combined with additional training and passed the examination required to practise at the Conseil d'Etat and the Cour de Cassation.

4. NOTARIES ('NOTAIRES')

As both a public law officer—because they hold the state seal—and an official appointee—because they hold an "office" awarded by the public authorities—the notary's role is to record documents that the parties must or wish to have certified as authentic.

Notaries therefore authenticate documents that must be officially certified in order to be valid, such as gifts, charges on immovable property, sales of property off-plan and documents that must be authenticated for land registration purposes, such as conveyances or transfers of immovable assets through inheritance.

The notarial code of ethics specific to the profession entails an obligation to act neutrally and impartially. A notary is more a jurist or legal expert on a file than his client's adviser. Moreover, he can be held criminally liable by all signatories of a document. His role is in some sense to mediate amicable solutions, serving the public interest in non-contentious matters.

In some parts of France, notaries also work in the real-estate sector, providing expert appraisals, conducting negotiations and in some cases, offering administrative services.

More and more notaries are responding to our society's increasing need to prevent matters from being litigated. They specialize in alternative dispute resolution methods, such as conciliation, mediation and even arbitration, in some fields.

There is a fixed scale of fees that notaries are permitted to charge for all activities that must be carried out by a member of the profession (property transactions and family-related matters). They are free to set their own fees in areas where there is competition for the work, notably company-corporate documents.

The specific nature of the notary's role has a direct influence on how people are recruited into the profession.

There are two main options—the academic route and the professional route, as well as a so-called social route—to become qualified as a notary, following several years of experience and a test of aptitude.

The academic route is open to students with a Master in law, by taking a Master's 2 course in "Notarial practice", followed by a two--year sandwich course. Future notaries are employed as interns in a notary's office, while following a course with four half-year modules, focusing on notarial matters. Access to the academic route is based on submitting an application and evaluation of the file.

The professional route is a parallel option and begins after completing a Master in law. Following the reform of 13 March 2013, access to this route is now also based on submitting an application. It consists of a 30-month sandwich course, consisting of six modules, each assessed by a national examination.

Students who opt for either of these routes must submit a report at the end of the course, and defend it before a panel of examiners. If successful, the candidate is delivered a diploma of notary.

Alongside the academic and professional routes, it is also possible to take a vocational degree in notarial practice. This is a three--year course, leading to qualification as a notary's clerk and it can provide a pathway to a Master in notarial practice and access to a postgraduate level.

Once qualified, a notary who wishes to practise must either buy an individual notary's practice or purchase shares in a partnership, or pass the national competitive examination organised each year to have access to an existing office.

5. BAILIFFS ('HUISSIERS')

Court bailiffs ('huissiers de justice') have a monopoly on serving extrajudicial (notices, orders, demands, etc.) or procedural documents (summons, seizures, etc.) and implementing court decisions and other enforceable instruments (seizures, expulsions, etc.). They can also carryout factual reports at the request of a judge or individual, and recover debts.

Bailiffs may also be chosen to take part in court hearings: calling cases, keeping order during the hearing and serving court documents (exchanged between barristers): in this case, they are known as ushers ('huissiers audienciers').

A law of 9 July 2015 provides for the creation of a new profession: the new 'commissaires de justice' will combine the functions of the court bailiff and court auctioneer ('commissaire-priseur judiciaire'). Along with their duties as bailiffs, they will also take on the responsibilities previously covered by legal auctioneers: expert appraisal, valuation and sale by public auction of furniture and moveable effects.

Court bailiffs hold an official appointment or are partners in a firm that holds one, and are authorised to practise by the Ministry of Justice, based on the documentation they submit. If they practise as individuals, they must either be appointed to a newly created office, or take over a firm after the existing holder ceases to practise.

Candidates must be of French nationality, hold a Master in law or an equivalent qualification and have passed the vocational court bailiff's examination after a two-year internship in a bailiff's office, alongside a training course attended at the École nationale de procédure.

Legal auctioneers, who were also publicly appointed legal officers, were recruited from holders of a Master in law and a qualification in the history of art as well as a vocational examination following the end of a two-year internship in an office.

6. CORPORATE LAWYERS

Corporate lawyers "who carry out their duties under an employment contract with a company or group of companies may, in carrying out these duties, and exclusively for the company that employs them, offer legal consultations and draft acts under private signature relating to the activities of said companies" (Act of 31 December 1990).

Unlike other members of the legal profession, corporate lawyers are not bound by codes of ethics and as the legislation stands, they cannot currently rely on the confidentiality of professional information, which is one of their demands.

The areas in which corporate lawyers practise are defined by their employment contract and depend largely on the size and activities of the company that employs them. While a large corporation may employ lawyers who specialise in a particular branch of the law, a small or medium-sized enterprise (SME) may only have one who, albeit with the support of external advisers, will be asked to draft contracts, prepare for general meetings, monitor disputes, deal with debt recovery, etc.

While the law does not set any conditions in terms of qualifications, in practice corporate lawyers generally have a postgraduate qualification (Master 2) in law. Several universities offer courses that combine law, management and accounting to better prepare potential candidates for the complexity and variety of the duties they will be asked to carry out.

CHAPTER FIVE

CRIMINAL LAW

1. SUBSTANTIVE CRIMINAL LAW

French criminal law, like most Western criminal systems, hesitates between two concepts when it comes to defining criminality.

One is objective, and defines the offence in relation to a given behaviour, which is viewed as a criminal act, regardless of the person who has committed it.

The other is subjective, and defines the offence with reference to the person who has committed it and their criminal tendencies. In the first case, the legislature, which is responsible for determining what constitutes an offence in tangible terms, determines the crime; in the second case, it is primarily concerned with the criminal. The consequences for the concept of criminal law itself are important.

While the Criminal Code of 1810 was broadly characterised by a mainly objective conception, it was possible to discern some degree of influence from a subjective analysis, primarily in the definition of the offence but also in the conception of the punishment. Since then, French criminal law has therefore been a hybrid. All subsequent developments, including the reform of the Criminal Code in 1992, have simply reinforced this characteristic, by accentuating the influence, however, of the subjective approach to criminal law.

This hybrid nature of French criminal law today shows that it is mainly objective at the point of defining offences, but is nonetheless tempered by subjective considerations. Conversely, it has become primarily subjective in its conception of punishment, although the original objective approach to punishment has not been entirely lost.

This objective conception of offences essentially views a crime as an act that has been declared unlawful because of the disturbance of public order it engenders. Such an approach focuses on tangible elements and the result of the offence. That said, alongside the tangible aspects of the offence, there is what is considered the moral or psychological element of the crime, the "*mens rea*" or criminal mindset of English-speaking legal systems, as opposed to the "*actus rea*" or criminal act. This attention paid to the criminal misconduct, intention or negligence, and therefore the psychology of the perpetrator, reflects the unquestionable influence of the subjective conception in defining offences. This inclusion of the psychological element has been accompanied, accordingly, by a decline in the importance of the result, with an increase in the number of statutory and formal offences; these are characterised by the fact that they are classified as offences regardless of the actual result, which often means criminalising situations that are simply dangerous.

The influence of the subjective approach to offences is even more apparent if we examine the second component of the offence, namely punishment. Although punishment, as described in abstract terms in criminal legislation, remains closely associated with the objective conception, both in its definition and with regard to the functions assigned to it, this ceases to be the case when it comes to deciding on the punishment to which the offender will actually be sentenced. Subjective considerations relating to the personality of the delinquent then come to the fore, to the point where punishments that are expressed in the law in abstract terms become technical reference mechanisms, which allow the offence to be classified as a serious crime ('crime'), major offence ('délit') or minor offence ('contravention') and determine the applicable system of law, even though it may not necessarily be applied.

As a result of these developments, contemporary French criminal law is very similar to other Western criminal laws derived from the Romano-Germanic system. If we put to one side the unusual position criminal law occupies in the legal disciplines in the French legal system, since in France it is still classified as private law, despite falling under public law in many other countries yet belonging to the same system of law, as for the rest, it is largely based on the underlying principles common to the major democratic legal systems.

The principle of legality remains a fundamental element with all the consequences it brings, notably with regard to the rules that govern the application of the law over time, enshrining the principle of the non-retroactive effect of more severe criminal laws and the necessity of a strict interpretation of criminal legislation. Unfortunately, this principle that is so essential in a democratic society is suffering a certain decline, associated on the one hand, with a fall in the quality of the law, which is often poorly drafted and gives rise to an interpretation of criminal definitions that can sometimes appear to rely on intuition, and on the other, the recent Europeanisation of the discipline, which is now subject to a superior source of law against which domestic provisions must be measured. This development has resulted in an increase in the powers of the criminal judge, who is now responsible for verifying the compliance of French law, notably with the provisions of the European Convention for the Protection of Human Rights and Fundamental Freedoms.

Contemporary French criminal law is now embodied in a new Criminal Code, which is derived from four statutes of 22 July 1992. It entered into effect on 1 March 1994. The new Code is organised on the basis of a plan, so that it begins by dealing with the general theory of the law, followed by criminal responsibility and finally punishments, continuing with an examination of offences against persons, offences against property and, finally, offences against the

Nation, State and public peace. Although the Code is fairly traditional overall, it contains two major innovations, enshrining the notion of criminal responsibility of legal entities and taking error of law into consideration as a cause of criminal justification. The period after the 1992 Criminal Code came into effect was characterised by the promulgation of numerous criminal laws, notably that of 10 July 2000, which aimed to redefine the criminal offence of negligence, thereby challenging the fundamental unity that had existed until then, between the criminal offence of negligence and a civil fault. Finally, under the influence of the "law and order" ideology implemented some 20 years ago in the United States, France has embarked on a "zero tolerance" security policy, which may prove dangerous by jeopardising the fragile balance that criminal law must strike between defending society and protecting individual freedoms. However, the latest trends in criminal policy appear to suggest a desire to rethink the approach, limiting the use of imprisonment of offenders, which is deemed ineffective and scarcely propitious to the rehabilitation of those convicted.

2. CRIMINAL PROCEDURE

The aim and purpose of criminal procedure is to establish the rules used to investigate, prosecute and judge the perpetrators of criminal offences defined mainly in the Criminal Code, while reconciling the principles of freedom and security. The Code of Criminal Procedure, which brings all of these rules together, includes—exceptionally—a preliminary article that sets out the "philosophy", the essential principles contained in the French constitutional foundation, which must be respected in response to the demands of a democratic society. In this respect, the contribution and influence of European Union law are not insignificant, notably with the concept of a "fair trial" defined by the European Convention for the Protection of Human Rights and Fundamental Freedoms. These same principles, and ensuring that they are respected in the law used as the basis for prosecution, allow those on trial to refer the matter to the judge for verification of their compliance with the European Convention on Human Rights or the Constitution (by means of a priority question on constitutionality). They also allow a case to be referred to and therefore examined by the European Court of Human Rights, which acts as the Supreme Court in such matters. According to the preliminary article, criminal procedure must be "fair and adversarial and preserve a balance between the rights of the parties. It must guarantee a separation between those authorities responsible for prosecuting and those responsible for judging (. . .)." Moreover, it asserts the right of victims, the presumption of innocence and the right for the defendant to be informed of the charges against him and to be assisted by a defence lawyer. These principles must be applied throughout the proceedings where an individual's criminal liability is in question.

Criminal procedure determines the conditions under which someone can be questioned as part of the investigation, by which authorities and on which grounds, to avoid arbitrary decisions. It also specifies the circumstances under which someone can be held in custody (against his will) by the police or gendarmerie, their right to silence, their right to lie, their right to legal assistance and access to their case file, etc. Until recently, criminal procedure at the investigative stage did not meet the requirement for both sides to be represented, prioritising the idea of the inquisitorial system where the "suspect" was alone, with no information and no defence lawyer, to secure the supreme form of evidence, namely a confession. Today, a different approach has been adopted, which respects the balance between the parties through hearing both sides. The same principles apply in a free hearing, when someone is questioned by the police or gendarmerie; the interviewee can leave when he wishes, choose to remain silent and be assisted by a lawyer; he is also entitled to an interpreter. An investigation is always carried out under the control of the state prosecutor ('procureur de la République') and is generally sufficient to establish the facts of the case and allow the person to be brought to court for trial. The person concerned will receive a summons to be tried on a given date. Sometimes, however, because the case is more complicated or concerns a serious crime (such as murder or rape), a further inquiry is required and it is handed over to an investigating judge ('juge d'instruction'). The investigating judge is a member of the (sitting on the bench) judiciary, a judicial authority and a professional judge, whose independence and status are guaranteed by the constitution; the state prosecutor, on the other hand, who is also a professional judge (standing judge when addressing the bench), has not been recognised as having the status of a judicial authority by the European Court of Human Rights.

The investigative system is still largely inquisitorial, although adversarial elements and equal rights for the parties are becoming more widespread. The investigating judge acts as both investigator and judge during the investigative stage; it investigates the cases put forward by both the prosecution and the defence, but does not arbitrate between them, even though, today, he no longer has the power to detain people, since this role has been devolved to another independent judge, the 'liberty and custody judge' ('juge des libertés et de la détention'). The investigating judge has the power to question someone who is brought before him as being likely to have committed a serious crime or other major offence. He can also, if the facts are less clear, make the person concerned an 'assisted witness' ('témoin assisté'). In any event, the person will have access to his file; he will be assisted by a lawyer and, if necessary, an interpreter; he can challenge his indictment before an appeal court; he can request to have his testimony compared with others and for investigations to be ordered. At the end of this investigation, the investigating judge will inform the public prosecutor's office and the suspect that he deems the investigation to be complete, which will entitle them to ask for further investigations. The state prosecutor will classify the offence being prosecuted and ask for the suspect to be referred to the criminal court ('tribunal correctionnel') or 'cour d'assises' (for more serious offences). The suspect will put forward his argument and then the investigating judge will take his decision independently, either referring the case to court or not, having had the opportunity to revisit the facts and abandon certain charges or facts.

In principle, judgments are handed down by a bench; normally there are three judges, all of whom are independent professional judges. Minor offences are judged by a single judge; more serious crimes are sent to the 'cour d'assises' for trial by jury. The procedure there is adversarial, with the prosecution case made by the state prosecutor and the defence by barristers-attorneys. The victims or so-called "civil parties" also have legal representation. Judges must provide the grounds for their decision and discharge or acquit where the defendant's guilt is in doubt. Judgments may be referred to the court of appeal, which is also made up of independent professional judges, with the same guarantees as in the lower courts. Appeals may also be lodged with the Cour de Cassation, which will have a suspensive effect, or subsequently with the European Court of Human Rights.

CHAPTER SIX

PERSONS

A person is a subject with the capacity to hold rights and be subject to obligations. It is distinct from an object, over which the person can exercise power.

1. DISTINCTION BETWEEN NATURAL PERSONS AND JURIDICAL PERSONS-LEGAL ENTITIES

Natural persons, i.e. human beings, are automatically recognised as having legal personality. The notion of legal personality has sometimes been extended to abstract entities, which have no biological reality, i.e. legal entities consisting of groups of people or things, organised to carry out a particular task. The "physical" difference between natural persons and juridical persons explains why the rules on these two categories of persons are not strictly identical, particularly with regard to the start and end of legal personality.

In principle, legal personality is acquired when a human being is born. Until then, the child cannot be separated as an individual from the mother; the child is an integral part of her biological system. The child only acquires legal personality if he is born alive and viable. In exceptional situations, the law recognises that simply by having been conceived, the child has the possibility of acquiring rights whenever it is in his best interest *(infans conceptus pro nato habetur quoties de commodis ejus agitur)*. A conceived child can therefore receive an inheritance or gift, but cannot be subject to obligations. In order to acquire rights from conception, again the child needs to be born alive and viable.

Legal personality ends with the person's physical death. Civil death, which used to apply to certain offenders serving life sentences, by depriving them of legal personality, disappeared in 1854. Physical death is a biological fact which can be medically confirmed. It transforms the human being into a thing that must be treated with respect (Civ. Code, art. 16-1-1). In France, there is no subjective right that allows an individual to demand euthanasia.

Unlike natural persons, whose legal personality is acquired and disappears automatically at birth and upon death, legal entities or juridical persons must be created to exist and dissolved to disappear. Often, it is the legislature that expressly recognises the legal personality of certain groups. Nonetheless, legal personality can, independently of any legislative intervention, apply to "any group that has the ability to express a collective opinion for the defence of lawful interests, which are therefore worthy of judicial recognition and protection" (Cass. 2nd civ. ch., 28 January 1954). There are different kinds of legal entities. They exist in both public law (for example, the state, territorial communities and public institutions) and in private law. Legal entities under private law can be either groups of people (such as companies- corporations, associations, trade unions or economic interest groups) or a collection of assets (such as foundations).

The start of legal personality varies significantly, depending on the group. In some cases (for example, a co-owners' association), the will of the people who have created it is sufficient; other cases require some form of state authorisation, which varies according to the type of group. For example, a corporation or company needs to be registered on the Trade and Companies Register in order to acquire legal personality, while a non-profit association needs to be registered with the prefecture and a foundation requires a decree to be issued by the Conseil d'Etat, recognising its public benefit.

Legal personality ends when the group is dissolved and liquidated. Indeed, unlike natural persons whose legal personality disappears instantly at the time of death, legal entities survive the dissolution process for liquidation purposes.

A person's 'civil status' encompasses all the legal features associated with a person, that identify that person as an individual in society and to which the law attaches legal effects (e.g. capacity linked to attaining the age of majority, or the rights and obligations of spouses).

There are many elements that identify a natural person, which are consistent with the inherent features of the individual (nationality, sex, last name and first name, address) or associated with the family relationships (e.g. spouse, filiation). Nationality attaches someone to a state; their last name is used to indicate who the person is (and may be the father's or mother's name or a combination of the two, as the parents decide when the child is born), the sex to distinguish one from the other sex and the home address.

As an instrument of civil administration, civil status is recorded in formal documents, produced or completed whenever there is a significant event in someone's life (birth, death, marriage, etc.) and held as part of the public records. Civil status documents are officially recorded on registers and produced by registrars who are public law officers.

Some of the elements used to identify legal entities are shared with natural persons, such as their name, address (registered office) and nationality. These elements are strictly regulated by law and are similar to the civil status of natural persons, but do not have the same scope. The elements used to identify a legal entity always depend, in fact, on a statement of the will or wills, unlike the civil status of natural persons, which is to a large extent, removed from any decision-making and more a matter of public order.

Inalienability and imprescriptibility are thus two characteristics associated with the status of natural persons. Inalienability prohibits the person from changing their status through assignment or abandonment, in a way that contradicts reality. Otherwise, their status would no longer reflect reality. Imprescriptibility removes the civil status from the action of time: a civil status cannot be acquired or lost over any length of time. Today, these characteristics have been weakened. Thus, for example, acquiring the name of a natural person can be time-barred and granted as a result of fair possession over an extended period.

Capacity consists of a person's aptitude to acquire and exercise a right.

In principle, any natural person has capacity. A lack of capacity is exceptional; it is never total, as this would be equivalent to an absence of legal personality. There are two kinds of incapacity. Incapacity to hold rights prevents someone from becoming the holder of a particular right by depriving that person of its enjoyment (for example, the ban on minors disposing of their assets gratuitously); incapacity to exercise rights prevents someone from exercising a right, even though they hold it. The incapacity to exercise rights applies to unemancipated minors and adults who are protected by law because of a mental impairment (Civ. Code, art. 1124). A minor will be represented by his parents or, if both are deceased or deprived of parental authority, by a guardian acting in their place. An adult who lacks capacity, depending on the extent of their impairment, will be placed under judicial protection or given a curator or tutor-guardian. Judicial protection is the least onerous of the protection schemes: it applies to an adult who needs to be temporarily protected in relation to acts of civil life (Civ. Code, art. 433). The adult retains the ability to exercise his rights and can continue to manage his own assets but, *a posteriori*, his acts may be set aside on grounds of financial harm, lesion. Curatorship is suitable for an adult who, although not incapable of acting on his own behalf, needs to be assisted by a third party, the 'curateur,' (curator) for major acts of civil life (Civ. Code, art. 440). An adult who is placed under curatorship acts on his own and the assistance from the curator is confirmed by the curator's signature, next to his, on important documents relating to their assets, namely acts of disposition that impact the patrimony. An adult who is placed under tutorship-guardianship is someone with a more profound level of mental impairment, which means that he is represented on an ongoing basis by a 'tuteur' who will act on his behalf in acts of civil life (Civ. Code, art. 440). The tutor cannot enter into transactions that dispose of rights without prior authorisation from the family council or the judge of tutorships (Civ. Code, art. 505). Unlike judicial protection, curatorship and tutorship cannot be initiated without a court decision. In order to avoid court intervention, an individual can, in advance, provided he has not been placed under tutorship, make arrangements for his protection by a third party, for the time when he will no longer be able to look after his own interests, by entering into a kind of power of attorney called a 'mandat de protection future' (Civ. Code, art. 477).

Even if the person is not incapable, she can be protected on an ad hoc basis, if she is affected by a mental impairment. In practice, since capacity for entering into a contract is a condition for the validity of agreements, (Civ. Code, new art. 1128), a contract entered into when the individual is suffering from a mental illness can be cancelled as provided in articles 414-1 and 2 of the Civil Code.

The ability to acquire and exercise a right is often the reason for creating a legal entity. It allows it to own assets that are separate from the assets of its members. Legal entities exercise their rights through the bodies that represent them. The capacity to hold rights varies from one group to another, depending on their nature, purpose and form. In general terms, according to the principle of speciality, a legal entity can only act to fulfil its objects. New article 1145 of the Civil Code thus stipulates that "the capacity of juridical persons is restricted to the acts useful for the achievement of their purpose as defined by their bylaws and to the acts which are their accessories". Moreover, the law specifically provides for variations in the extent of legal personality, depending on the nature of the group: non-profit associations, for example, have only a "limited personality" insofar as they cannot receive assets gratuitously, except for manual gifts. An association that is recognised as offering a public benefit has a more "extensive personality", which allows it to acquire assets gratuitously without any restriction. Any legal entity, however restricted its capacity may be, will always have the right to take part in court proceedings to defend its interests.

2. RIGHTS ATTACHED TO PERSONALITY

Rights attached to personality are the rights inherent in persons which allow them to defend their integrity. They are attached to the person and are outside the patrimony (non-transferable, unseizable and not subject to prescription) and enforceable vis-à-vis all. A natural person has the right to protection from physical and mental prejudice from birth. While it is not possible to grant a legal entity the right to protection of its physical integrity, because of its disembodied nature, protection of its moral integrity can be recognised.

Article 16-1 of the Civil Code provides that "everyone has the right to respect for his body". Two principles are involved in guaranteeing such respect. The principle of inviolability of the human body prohibits third parties from committing unjustified interference with physical integrity causing bodily harm. Such interference is, in practice, only permitted on the twofold condition that the person committing it has secured the person's prior consent and is pursuing a legitimate end, as provided for in law (for example, medical or research purposes). The condition of consent protects the person concerned from third parties, who must accept their refusal; the condition of purpose protects them from themselves, so that they are not tempted to consent to an intervention that would be harmful to them.

The principle that the human body is not a part of the patrimony, prevents the body or part of the body being handed over to another person for money. It is an element of the principle, established in case law, of the inalienability of the human body, to which it is closely related, and which opposes any disposal of the body, even gratuitously. It should be noted that the body as a whole cannot be handed over to another person, either gratuitously or against payment, although specific parts of the body can be donated (for example, organ or blood donation).

Moral integrity also relates to the "incorporeal" or intangible elements of the person, which define them in their relationship to other people: honour, but also voice, image, innocence, private life, etc. The various rights attached to these elements all share a common nature and structure, insofar as they oblige a third party to seek the person's consent before doing anything that would affect a person's moral integrity. We must observe, however, that moral integrity is less well protected today than it was in the past. Attempts against which an individual has not given her consent are no longer systematically punished. The protection of moral integrity frequently gives way to freedom of expression and information when a public person or body is involved. Only dignity, which opposes any subjugation or degradation of the human person, is likely to curb such a decline, by preventing any attempt against moral integrity, even when consent is granted.

CHAPTER SEVEN

THE FAMILY

1. CONJUGAL UNIONS

There are three kinds of conjugal unions in French law.

Marriage can only be a civil act: no religious marriage can be celebrated unless it has first been performed in city hall (based on the ideal of secularity inherited from the 1789 Revolution). Since 2014, both homosexual and heterosexual marriages have been allowed. The minimum age is 18. Bigamy is strictly prohibited, as is incest between ascendant and descendant relatives and between brother and sister. The spouses' consent must be real: sham marriage, i.e. marriage to secure a result that is unrelated to matrimony (such as obtaining a residence permit) is null and void.

On a *personal* level, spouses are subject to duties of fidelity, assistance (as a moral concept), cohabitation and respect (any form of domestic violence is condemned). On a *pecuniary* level, they are bound by a duty to provide support (of a maintenance nature); debts contracted, either together or separately, to maintain the household or educate the children, bind both spouses solidarily vis-à-vis third parties; they can only dispose jointly of the rights that provide accommodation for the family (such as selling their apartment or terminating a lease agreement). All these effects of marriage are of public order.

On the other hand, the principle of freedom in matrimonial agreements allows the couple to agree on the arrangements for their respective contributions to the costs of the marriage and the status of their property. If there is no agreed upon prenuptial agreement (which is the case for 90% of couples), they contribute to the expenses of the marriage according to their respective ability and their matrimonial regime is that of the *community property ('communauté d'acquêts').* Under this regime, assets acquired against payment during the marriage are their joint property, while those acquired before the marriage or received through inheritance or donation are their own property. Jointly owned assets are shared equally when the matrimonial regime is dissolved. The joint property serves as security for each of the spouses' creditors, except where there are rules that protect joint assets from borrowing or being used as security. They are managed on the basis of strict equality: both in terms of *interdependence* (i.e. a system of concurrent management, which is the principle that each of the spouses can act alone), *association* (i.e. a system of joint management, which is required for major transactions, such as selling an immovable, making a donation or taking out a mortgage, where the couple must act jointly), and *independence* (i.e. a system of exclusive management, which replaces concurrent management in relation to assets assigned to the exercise of a separate profession: only one of the spouses is able to act). The couple may opt for a different matrimonial regime by entering into a prenuptial agreement, which must be drawn up by a notary: wider community property (for example, universal community, which includes all the spouses' assets), separation of property (where each spouse retains exclusive ownership of the property they acquire) or sharing in the acquêts (acquisitions) ('participation aux acquêts') (if the marriage is dissolved, the spouse who has acquired fewer assets can claim a sum of money equal to half the difference from the other). It is possible to change a matrimonial regime during the marriage, subject to the approval of the court where there are minor children, or if the switch is opposed by an adult child or creditor. The most common changes are opting for universal community of property, where everything reverts to the surviving spouse so as to secure his/her financial situation, or separation of property, to protect one spouse from the business liabilities of the other.

Civil partnership (partenariat) was introduced in France in 1989 with the *pacte civil de solidarité* (civil pact of solidarity). Originally designed as a legal and financial regime for homosexual couples, who were prohibited from marrying at the time, it has undergone two major changes: legally, it has come closer to marriage, with a reform in 2004 attaching personal effects to it; in practice, 90% of couples who enter a civil partnership today are heterosexual. A civil partnership-civil pact of solidarity is entered into in writing, either as an agreement under private signature or drawn up as an authentic act; either way it must be recorded at the registry of the local court. Its effects are broadly similar to those of a marriage, except that on a personal level a civil partnership does not impose a duty of fidelity; on a patrimonial level, there is no requirement for joint management of the partners' home; and in terms of their assets, each partner retains ownership of their own, similar to a married couple under a regime of separation of property, unless they agree to adopt a regime of ownership in indivision, which is a more restricted form of community property. A civil pact of solidarity can be easily amended.

Cohabitation, *concubinage*, is simply defined by the Civil Code as a de facto union of an heterosexual or homosexual couple, living together on a stable and continuous basis. It does not produce the effects of either a marriage or a civil partnership: is a 'free union.' However, the law does grant some rights to the cohabitees or partners (for example, in relation to residential leases or welfare benefits) and case law recognises them some rights that they may derive from resorting to the ordinary law (for example, the theory of unjustified enrichment or the theory of de facto creation of a company, which allows a cohabitee who has contributed to the other's profession to claim either a right to compensation or a right to the company's assets).

2. DISSOLUTION OF UNIONS

Marriage is dissolved by death or divorce (around 45%). Divorce is characterised by multiple causes, the disassociation of its causes and effects, the contractualisation of its effects and the concentration of its effect in time.

There are four types of divorces: 1) *Divorce by mutual consent* implies the spouses' agreement *to* both the principle *and* the consequences of their separation. It is a judicial procedure: divorce is pronounced by the judge, after the court has ascertained that the agreement governing its ultimate consequences is in accordance with the interests of both the couple and their children. The procedure can take as little as a few months. 2) *Uncontested divorce* again implies the spouses' consent, but this is limited to the principle of their separation. The judge records the agreement but decides what will happen after the divorce. 3) *Fault-based divorce* (divorce—matrimonial offence with breakdown of the marriage) implies a serious and repeated breach of the duties of marriage, to the extent that continuing to live together is no longer tolerable: the reality of the breach is assessed by the judge (there are no longer any faults that are deemed absolute grounds for divorce, i.e. circumstances which, as used to be the case with adultery, oblige the judge to pronounce a divorce). 4) *Divorce for irretrievable breakdown of the marital relationship* (divorce based on breakdown which may be a divorce by repudiation) requires the separation of the couple for at least two years: once the separation has been established, the judge must pronounce the divorce.

The effects of divorce are independent from its cause. The fact that one of the spouses has committed a fault is therefore of no consequence.

In addition to the case of mutual consent, the law encourages the spouses to reach an agreement on all or some of the effects of their divorce. Their agreements are subject to confirmation by the judge.

Divorce can result in a compensatory allowance designed to offset, as far as possible, the disparity created in the spouses' respective living conditions. This is not a maintenance payment (which can be revised and may be subject to payment incidents): in principle, it is paid as a lump sum and is intangible.

The effects of the marriage can be lessened without it being dissolved, if the couple decide to separate, which the judge can pronounce under the same circumstances as a divorce. The duty to live together ceases; the contribution to the expenses of the marriage takes the form of a maintenance payment, which can be revised and is payable by the spouse who is better off; if applicable, the system of community property can be replaced by a separation of property.

A civil partnership is dissolved by the death or the marriage of one of the partners, their mutual consent or a unilateral declaration by one of them: no judge is involved. No compensatory allowance is paid. In simple terms, a separation resulting from a fault may render the perpetrator delictually liable.

Cohabitation ends with an agreed or unilateral *de facto* termination of living together. In case of violence, leading to termination of the cohabitation, there may be a ground for delictual liability.

3. FILIATION AND PARENTAGE

The principle of equality has led to any distinction between children based on the circumstances of their birth being abandoned: even the terms *legitimate* filiation and *natural* filiation have disappeared from the law. In terms of its establishment, paternal or maternal filiation is established either by the birth certificate, or by recognition, or by the possession of status (which is an apparent filiation created by the name used, the behaviour of the parties concerned, treating each other as parent and child, and by the belief of third parties, such as the administrative authorities), or by a judgment accepting an action to record filiation. Moreover, if the child is born to a married woman, the husband's paternity is presumed: the only remaining vestige of the distinction between legitimate filiation and natural filiation. Actions to record or contest filiation are time-barred after 30 years, and sometimes less. As far as the *effects* of filiation are concerned, all children have the same rights and the same obligations.

There are two forms of adoptive filiation. *Full* adoption involves substituting one family for another: it brings the child fully into their adoptive family and removes him from his original family. Aiming to give a family to a child or a child to a family, it requires that the child be less than 15 years old and the parents be at least 15 years older. *Simple* adoption effectively adds a family: the child joins his adoptive family but remains a member of his blood or natural family. It is often done for inheritance purposes. There is no age restriction. Both forms of adoption are available to single persons (individual adoption) or to married heterosexual or homosexual couples (marital adoption) but not to civil partners or cohabitees. The adoption of a spouse's child, which is frequent in families that have reconstituted or blended following death or divorce, is subject to specific rules.

Endogenous or exogenous medically assisted reproduction (i.e. with or without a third-party donor, who remains strictly anonymous) is permitted but strictly regulated. It is only available to heterosexual couples who are married, civil partners or cohabitees, and of child-bearing age: a homosexual couple is therefore not able to use the procedure and any insemination, fertilisation or implantation *post mortem* is prohibited. Establishing the child's filiation is governed by particular rules.

Surrogacy agreements are prohibited, regardless of whether the mother bearing the child is the genetic mother or not. However, a child born in a country where surrogacy agreements are allowed, and where his filiation has been officially established, can have the foreign document transcribed into French civil status records.

The rights and obligations of parents are no longer dependent on their situation, whether they are married, civil partners, divorced or separated.

They have an obligation to provide for the care of the child, that may extend into adulthood (for example, if they are continuing their studies).

They are vested with parental authority, which has both a personal feature, (the child's education and protection) and a pecuniary feature (administering the child's assets). Parental authority is exercised jointly, at least in principle, even if they are separated. In the latter case, the child's home is determined either by agreement, or by the court: it can alternate (one week with one parent, and the other week with the other). Parental authority is inalienable: parents cannot disregard their duty. *Delegation* to a third party is, however, possible, under the control of the court: it may be total or partial, and either transfer or share the attached prerogatives (for example, shared parental authority with a new spouse). Parents who neglect their parental duties risk having their authority *withdrawn* by the court.

4. SUCCESSIONS

Succession is governed by statute or testament. The law classifies the relatives of the deceased in four hierarchical categories: 1) descendants; 2) immediate ascendants (father and mother) and immediate collateral relatives (brothers and sisters and their descendants); 3) ordinary ascendants; 4) ordinary collateral relatives. Within each category, the closer relative excludes those who are more distant and heirs of the same degree of closeness inherit per capita, except in the case of *representation* in the category of descendants and close collateral relatives (an heir who has predeceased the deceased person or an heir who renounces the inheritance or is unworthy is represented by his descendants, who are substituted for him) and *distribution by line* in the categories of ordinary ascendants and collateral relatives (half each for the paternal and maternal lines, then classification in each line, depending on the degree of closeness). Where there are descendants, the spouse receives a quarter of the estate in ownership or the whole estate in usufruct if all the children are the couple's, or a quarter in ownership otherwise; the spouse receives half or three quarters in ownership if the mother and father, or one of them, are still alive; the spouse excludes all other relatives, except that there is a right of reversion for brothers and sisters with respect of half of the property that the deceased had received from common ascendants. In addition, the spouse is entitled to a right for life to use and live in the property included in the estate which is his main home. Civil partners and cohabitees have no right to inherit.

Freedom to dispose gratuitously by gift or will—testament, is limited by a public order of succession, the main elements of which are the reserved portion (la réserve héréditaire) and the prohibition of agreements on the future estate of a living person. A *reserve* is granted to descendants (½, ⅔ or ¾ where there are one, two or three or more children) and if there are no descendants, to the spouse (¼). The réserve is based on all the assets that the deceased left at his death, plus all the assets he distributed inter vivos by gift. The *prohibition on agreements relating to future successions* prohibits: on the one hand, a presumptive heir from disposing of his rights to an inheritance that is not yet open (although there are an increasing number of exceptions, for example, it is possible to waive in advance, the right to bring an action to reduce a gift made to an individual during the deceased person's lifetime, when it would impinge on the reserved portion); on the other, the deceased from disposing of his succession by any means other than a will—testament (which is why the contractual appointment of an heir is null and void, except in the case of a prenuptial agreement or an agreement between the spouses during their marriage).

As regards the transfer of the succession, the heirs *acquire* their rights as soon as the person dies. They may also *exercise* their rights immediately, without a third—party administrator, since they have the saisine, i.e. the *right to take possession without formalities* (which is the case of all heirs and, under certain conditions, the universal legatee): this is an application of the principle of *continuation of the deceased person* or *succession to the person* (as opposed to *succession to assets*).

With regard to the liquidation of debts, universal heirs or heirs by universal title (who are destined to receive all or a share of the estate of the de cujus) are obliged to settle the debts of the estate *ultra vires successionis,* even if they exceed the value of the asset received: this is another application of the principle of continuation of the person of the deceased or succession to the person. They can, however, by only accepting the inheritance in the amount of the net assets, limit their obligation to settle the debts of the estate to the value of the asset received.

With regard to the liquidation of the assets, if there is no amicable settlement, under the law the court will arrange for them to be split, which involves a drawing of lots. The law does, however, allow for preferential allocations, which consist in attributing a particular item to a particular heir based on the importance it has for him (such as the home, or the business through which they earn their living) and also prevent any parcelling out that could be a mortal blow of an agricultural, commercial, industrial or professional business (the survival of which, on the death of the owner, is a major concern in contemporary inheritance law).

Finally, from a tax perspective, tax is payable on all inherited assets, except those falling to the spouse or civil partner (assuming, in the case of the latter, that he has been made the legatee).

CHAPTER EIGHT

PROPERTY

1. SCOPE OF PROPERTY

The concept of property—biens—things—encompasses everything that can be assigned a monetary value and can be included in an individual's patrimony. As a consequence, property includes not only corporeal things, movables or immovables, but also incorporeal things, i.e. incorporeal patrimonial rights, such as claims, shares, artisanal, professional or business concerns, copyrights, patents, trademarks, etc. Their common denominator is their pecuniary-patrimonial value. *Conversely,* so-called non-pecuniary or non-patrimonial rights, such as fundamental personal, civil and political rights, are not things or property.

Property—things—as defined in the Civil Code are first, things in the material sense of the term i.e. corporeal things, which are necessarily either movables or immovables.

Are *immovables* things and rights that have a direct link with land, i.e. the land itself, anything attached to the land (buildings, constructions and plantations) and all rights that are directly concerned with the same things. Although immovable ownership generally refers to the ownership of a plot of land, it also extends above and below it, within the imprecise limits of what is within human reach. All works, constructions, buildings or plantations, regardless of who created them, belong in principle, through accession, to the owner of the land. May also be an immovable thing the upper element only, separately from what is underneath (the acreage, the surface area), or an identifiable structure, separate from the land. The owner can object to any impingement or intrusion from the air or below ground. Water—both rainwater and water from springs, rivers and lakes—is governed by specific rules.

All other corporeal things are *movables*. Although animals have recently been acknowledged as "sentient living creatures" (Act of 16 February 2015) and are subject to particular protective rules, they are still treated, in legal terms, as movable things (Civ. Code, art. 515-14).

There are, however, various marginal exceptions to the physical criterion used to distinguish between immovable and movable things (such as movable things that are intended to become immovable by destination: immovable things that are treated as movables by anticipation).

Incorporeal things include all patrimonial rights with no physical substance, such as the right to receive payment of a debt and intellectual creations. While their patrimonial nature has never been in doubt, the Civil Code has largely ignored their status as things. The regulation of *claims* is largely governed by the law of obligations, while the regulation of *shares and marketable securities* falls under company law. *Intellectual creations* only began their remarkable rise, which has steadily increased, after the era of the 1804 Code and have been covered by specific legislative provisions, which explains why they receive only limited attention in books on the law of things—property. The digital era has opened a new chapter, with the creation of "virtual property", a new variety of incorporeal things.

Nonetheless, all these incorporeal patrimonial rights are still things, to which the ordinary law of things still applies, in principle. Claims are items of ownership. The same applies to the incorporeal things represented by business concerns and now, artisanal, professional and agricultural businesses, which can be described as "professional things." These are a way of valuing professional activities. It is important to note that, while they may include moveable corporeal things (such as merchandise and working tools), the immovable thing in which they are run is never part of it. This is even more true of intellectual creations, which have been recognised as property from the outset, i.e. literary and artistic property and industrial property (patents and trademarks). All of these things can be owned, subject to various transfers, become real sureties, etc., in the same way as corporeal things.

While all incorporeal rights are, *lato sensu,* intellectual rights, insofar as they are derived from legal techniques that are the fruit of human intellectual endeavour and not of the nature of things, the term "intellectual property" usually only applies to pure intellectual creations, such as literary and artistic works, and processes that have an industrial, commercial or professional purpose, such as patents, trademarks, designs, models and similar works.

The law recognises that authors, creators and artists have an exclusive patrimonial right to their works, in the form of a monopoly of using them as best as they can. Literary and artistic property rights deserve to be described as property insofar as they relate directly to its object, similar to the ownership of corporeal things. Such rights belong to the author or creator and pass down to their successors, but they are limited in time to the 70 years following the death of the author or creator. They are distinct from ownership of the artistic works themselves, which fall within the scope of legal transactions. Patrimonial rights are coupled with a non-patrimonial moral right, which is not classified as a thing, that is transferred under different rules and does not end.

The concept of industrial property is traditionally applied to patents, trademarks, designs and models. Specific provisions govern designations of origin, plant varieties, databases and software.

2. POWERS OVER THINGS

The law of things is based on two pillars: ownership and possession. While ownership—private or public—is the norm, and if things are generally appropriated, the owner also needs to be able to provide evidence of his right. However, in French law, there is no absolute evidence of ownership. The documents or titles the alleged owner may present, in relation to both immovables and movables, have only relative value and can be rebutted, even if they have been publicly recorded in some form, such as land registration. It is at this point that the de facto situation of possession comes to the owner's assistance, thanks to the effects associated with it.

Setting aside the alleged "absolutism" and the philosophical and political debates that have revolved around it, the right of ownership remains the right that grants its holder the maximum prerogatives it is possible to have in relation to a thing. It constitutes a right in rem, a real right, which gives its holder a direct and immediate right to the thing, which is enforceable against all third parties, as opposed to a personal right, such as the right to receive payment of a debt, which grants a right against another individual. It is the most comprehensive right in rem that exists, because of the three prerogatives attached to it, which are known as *usus, fructus* and *abusus.*

Usus is the right to use the property one owns, according to the specific nature of each thing: living in a building, cultivating land, using various objects, etc. *Usus* also implies, in negative terms, the right not to use something.

Fructus is the right to enjoyment, i.e. the right to the fruits of the appropriated thing, either directly, by taking the fruits it produces, or indirectly, by receiving the income earned from granting the right to use and enjoy it to someone else (payable as rent, interest, etc.).

Abusus, finally, is the right to dispose of the item, either physically, by consuming, transforming or destroying it, or legally, by transferring it inter vivos or mortis causa, or granting rights to it to third parties.

The prerogatives listed above can be divided along various levels, the components of which, usually described as attributes of ownership, also constitute distinct rights in rem, which may belong to different individuals.

The distinction between *usufruct* and *naked ownership* is the most common division. The holder of the usufruct is entitled to use and enjoy the thing, usually for life. The naked owner retains ownership of the property, minus the usufruct, with the intention of recovering full ownership once the usufruct expires. Both can dispose of their rights freely.

Other rights in rem include, though they are more limited in scope, *rights of use and/or habitation* and the various legal or conventional servitudes that may encumber a property to the benefit of another person. More recently, case law has recognised the possibility of establishing a simple, specific real right of enjoyment that is limited in time. This jurisprudence closes the old debate on the existence of a numerus clausus of real rights.

These real rights are called *principal* rights, insofar as they are useful to the holder in their own right, as opposed to accessory real rights or real securities, which are intended to guarantee a debt (see below).

Possession is the de facto situation of someone who holds something as its owner. It consists of two elements: *corpus* and *animus.*

Corpus refers to physically holding the object. *Animus* expresses the desire to appropriate it. Possession is therefore, in French law, distinct from simply holding or detention, something without any intent. Possession only exists where the possessor pretends to be the owner. As a result, someone who holds something on behalf of someone else, such as a tenant, borrower or depositary, is not a possessor. In these situations, the *corpus* is in the hands of the holder, but on behalf of the possessor, who is then said to possess it *solo animo,* i.e. only by intention.

Possession is said to be in good faith if the possessor believes he is the owner, notably as a result of having acquired the property from someone who described himself as owner. Conversely, the possessor is in bad faith if he claims to be the owner when he knows he is not. However, while good faith is always presumed, it is not a constituent element of possession, which produces certain effects, such as acquisitive prescription, even where there is bad faith.

Possession must meet certain criteria to produce these effects, i.e. it must be continuous (except for movable things), peaceful, public and unequivocal.

In strictly logical terms, the simple fact of possession should not produce any effect in law. However, the impossibility of producing absolute evidence of ownership—*probatio diabolica*—vests in possession a significant importance.

With respect to moveable property, it means that ownership is acquired instantly if it is in good faith. A limited right of revendication within three years is reserved to an owner who has been deprived of it by theft or loss. This rule means there is a high level of security and fluidity in the trade of movable property.

Regarding immoveable property, it means that ownership is presumed and thus relieves the owner or alleged owner, if he is in possession, from having to provide evidence of his right, placing the burden of proof to the contrary on the claimant. If it has lasted for a certain period of time without being contested, it also has the effect of making the owner's right unchallengeable: this is known as usucapion or prescriptive acquisition. The period is 10 years if the possessor acted in good faith and acquired under just title. It is 30 years in other cases, whether the possessor acted in good or bad faith. In certain cases, it thus allows a usurper to become the definitive owner, a solution that may seem shocking at first sight, but for which there are several possible justifications. Above all, it definitely strengthens the right of the true owner, who is released from worry around the impossibility of providing absolute evidence of his ownership.

However, this mechanism applies mainly to corporeal property.

3. USE OF THINGS FOR PURPOSES OF SECURITY

Using property to guarantee a debt is an idea as old as civilisation. Pledges and mortgages are the classic examples. The constant need for credit has resulted in a diversification of techniques, so that to make the principle applicable to all kinds of things, even incorporeal, and ultimately to ownership itself.

Some forms of securities can only apply to immoveable property, such as mortgage, which is recorded, and antichresis—now known as a "pledge of real property"—which involves dispossessing the debtor, but which is hardly used today.

Other forms of securities necessarily relate to movable things, such as the pledge, with or without dispossession of the debtor, for corporeal movable things, and pledge as a security on incorporeal things.

Other types of securities can apply equally either to movables and immovables: traditionally, these are various privileges recognised by the law as applying to certain classes of creditors. A later addition was ownership—security in two forms: retaining ownership to provide a guarantee (reservation of ownership clause) and ownership transferred as a guarantee or held as fiducia-security.

Real securities are mostly based on an agreement (pledge, mortgage or fiducia). They are sometimes created by law (such as mortgages or privileges) or more rarely, judicially created (mortgages or pledge of an incorporeal movable).

These are accessory rights in rem. As a prototype of the principal right in rem, ownership can therefore, paradoxically, act as an accessory real right.

4. DISPOSITION OF THINGS

Holders of principal rights in rem (excluding the right of usage and habitation, which are strictly personal, and servitudes which are attached to the dominant and servient estates), can, in principle, dispose freely of them (principle of free transferability), as illustrated by the creation of charges. According to the principle of consensualism, the transfer of an assigned right in rem takes place simply through an exchange of consent, without any other formality. It is only if the parties choose to defer it (notably for reasons of security rights), if an immediate transfer is impossible (because of a future or indeterminate object) or if the law decides otherwise, that this is not the case. The sole purpose of the registration process required for immoveable property is to make the transfer enforceable against third parties.

Parties to a contract or a gift, as well as the testator, may include a non-transferability clause, but it must be limited in time and justified by a serious and legitimate interest. Non-transferability also implies the impossibility of seizure by creditors.

In specified circumstances, non-transferability can also result from a legal provision or a court decision. In a particular situation, an individual business owner can even declare his principal residence or other non business-related immovable property to be unseizable (but not non-transferable).

CHAPTER NINE

CONTRACT

1. CONTRACT IN PRIVATE LAW

The main source of contractual law is in the Civil Code, in two successive sets of rules: the general rules applicable to all contracts, in Title III of Book III (art. 1101 to 1369-11) and, since 1 October 2016, when the broad reform of the law of contract came into force following the ordinnance of 10 February 2016, in articles 1100 to 1303-4; and the rules specific to each type of contract. Only the general rules are considered here.

There are other sources in addition to the Civil Code, for example, the Consumer Code. Above all, case law constitutes a significant source since, in practice, it has contributed to filling the gaps in the Civil Code in several important areas, including preliminary contracts, offer and acceptance, the duration or term of the contract, unilateral breach, assignment of contract, groups of contracts, etc.

The Civil Code initially conceived of the contract exclusively as a source of debts. This was the definition of a contract according to article 1101. The crucial moment was therefore the point at which the debtor was committed, which was conceived as instantaneous. What happens after the contract is entered into was combined with the regime of obligations (Chapter III, IV, V, VI).

The development of positive law gave the lie to this oversimplified view. A contract is not simply an instantaneous source of debts. On the one hand, it produces other legal effects, which vary depending on the nature of the contract. On the other, the formation of a contract often involves a series of steps, which give rise to various obligations, even before the parties enter into it.

The reform of the law of contract by the ordonnance of 10 February 2016 takes this development into account.

1.1. FORMATION

French law is based on a principle derived from Enlightenment philosophy: the autonomy of the will. This underpins two fundamental rules:

As regards the substance of the law of contract, it is the freedom of contract: this is the rule expressed in new article 1102 of the Civil Code. The parties determine which law should govern the contract at their discretion. Moreover, the law chosen governs only those who have agreed to it. This is the rule expressed in new article 1199 of the Civil Code. Their will cannot go against a law concerning public order and good morals (Civ. Code, art. 6). This degree of freedom has lessened as the concept of public order has grown since the end of the 19th century.

The parties are free to determine the form of their contract. This is the principle of consensualism (new art. 1172). However, this principle is tempered, first, by the requirements of proof: proof of a contract must, in principle, be constituted in advance if its value is higher than a certain amount (currently €1,500) by producing a notarised document or act under private signature (see Civ. Code, new art. 1359). Next, the principle is set aside by a number of provisions that require more or less burdensome formalities.

A contract is formed once there has been an exchange of consent; the debtor's commitment must be accepted by the creditor, failing which it can still be revoked.

Consent is protected from vices of consent; consumer law adds specific mechanisms related to protection. The formation of the contract may be preceded by a preliminary contract.

French law is torn between protecting the debtor and the need for the security of transactions. Three *vices of consent* have been preserved, each one leading to the nullity of a contract.

Fraud (dol-dolus) (new art. 1137 and 1138) is misleading the other party to the contract; it renders the contract null where it was a determining factor. Fraud-dolus (dol) is also a wrong, for which the perpetrator can be held liable. The scheme or manoeuvre may consist of positive action (such as lying or dissimulating) or silence (fraudulent non-disclosure), whenever one of the parties, particularly a professional, was under a duty to inform the other party to the contract spontaneously.

Duress-violence (new art. 1140 to 1143) is an illegitimate pressure intended to influence a party to a contract by the other party or a third party. It can be physical or psychological (threats, blackmail, etc.). It also implies carrying out an act of *duress-violence (abuse)* and cannot be solely the result of economic circumstances (if someone is in a state of necessity or economic dependence).

Error (new art. 1132 to 1136) : where a party made a mistake as to the matter of the agreement at the moment it gave its consent. As the other party has done nothing wrong, yet the contract will nonetheless be null, the nullity is subject to the essential and excusable nature of the error. Moreover, an error over the value of the prestation is excluded.

All three vices alter the integrity of the contractual will. Conversely, French law is not concerned with the economic balance of reciprocal prestations: lesion is not, except in certain circumstances (for example,: the sale of a building), a ground for the nullity of the contract (new art. 1168).

Consumer law has developed several *ex ante* mechanisms to protect the consumer's consent, such as the cooling-off or withdrawal period, a compulsory description of the product's or service's characteristics, a handwritten note confirming awareness of the commitment, etc.

A contract is formed when an offer is accepted (new art. 1113 to 1122).

An offer is a unilateral act, by which a person expresses his willingness to enter into a contract. It must be firm, accurate and complete. Failing this, it is simply an invitation to enter into negotiations. An offer is rendered null by the death of the offeror, or if the offeror becomes incapable or has his patrimony seized. It can be withdrawn: the contract can never be imposed on the offeror. The latter can, however, be obliged to provide compensation for the harm caused by his withdrawal.

Acceptance is also a unilateral act. It must be unconditional; failing this, it is a counter-offer. Acceptance must be expressed verbally or by unequivocal behaviour; the mere silence of the recipient does not, in principle, amount to an acceptance.

The contract is formed at the time and at the place where acceptance is received (new art. 1121).

Often, entering into the contract is preceded by a period of negotiations. During the negotiations, the parties may enter into various agreements (such as a letter of intent, non-disclosure agreements, agreement in principle, exclusivity agreement, etc.). Nonetheless, the end of negotiations is conclusive. If the negotiations break down because of the fault of the party concerned, it may be a ground for extracontractual/delictual liability; the harm suffered consists of the costs of negotiation incurred and lost by the victim, but not the fact of being deprived of the expected profits of the planned contract (new art. 1112).

Entering into the contract may be preceded by a preliminary contract. A *unilateral promise* to enter into a contract gives one of the parties, for a necessarily limited time, the right to opt for or against entering into the contract, at her discretion (new art. 1124). A *bilateral promise*, a synallagmatic promise which the Civil Code rightly does not mention, is fully binding on the parties pending a future event, upon which entering into the contract depends (such as a suspensive condition, a formality, etc.). A preferential agreement or *pacte de préférence* (pact of preference) (new art. 1123) is a simple preferential promise should the promissor decide to enter into a contract.

Several other conditions must be met in addition to the exchange of consent.

First, the contract must not be contrary to the norms concerning *public order* and good moral standards (Civ. Code, art. 6 and 1102, para. 2). The *purpose* of the contract must be lawful (new art. 1162).

Next, the *object* of the contractual obligation must be possible and certain, though not necessarily present (new. art. 1128-3.), determinable (new art. 1163) and lawful.

Until the 2016 reform, the obligation required a cause (old art. 1131), a somewhat obscure and controversial concept, which was used as a means of control of the rationality of the debtor's commitment.

1.2. PERFORMANCE-EXECUTION

Performance-execution is governed by two principles: binding force and relative effect of a contract.

The central legislation was previously article 1134 of the Civil Code, now articles 1103, 1104 and 1193, which set out three complementary rules:

- the imperial nature of the contract;
- the immutability of the contract;
- the performance-execution of the contract in good faith.

According to the principle of imperialism, the contract governs the parties' behaviour (new art. 1103), as the law itself does (it has "the force of law" for the parties). It is a law that is imposed on the parties. But it is also a law for the judge and third parties, who cannot contribute to breaching the contract.

Certain remedies for non-performance (art. 1217 to new art. 1231-7) are general, while others are specific to bilateral/synallagmatic contracts.

The *general remedies* are specific performance-forced execution (in nature or equivalent) and contractual liability. A creditor can obtain a remedy of specific performance-forced execution in nature against a debtor, except in a few limited cases (new art. 1221). He can also replace a debtor who is in breach (new art. 1222). The order may be accompanied by an astreinte or financial penalty (periodic penalty payment).

A creditor can also opt for performance by equivalent, in the form of damages; these can have been assessed in advance (Civ. Code, new art. 1231-5), even in the perspective of a threat. Otherwise, the amount of damages will consist in the loss suffered by the creditor and the profit of which he has been deprived (Civ. Code, new art. 1231-2) to the extent foreseeable at the time the debtor entered into the commitment, unless the non-performance (non--execution) is fraudulent (Civ. Code, new art. 1231-3). Waivers or clauses that limit liability are, in principle, effective (except in relationships between professionals and consumers) with the same exception. The debtor can rely on an exoneration clause, such as force majeure or the act of a third party or the creditor himself (Civ. Code, new art. 1218). The liability of the debtor requires the creditor to have proven the non-performance. This proof is easy where the obligor has promised to achieve a specific result (obligation of result) and not only the obligor's due diligence (obligation of means). In order to determine the non-performance of an obligation, new art. 1194 states to rely not only on what is stated in the agreement, but also on "all that follows" according to equity, usage and the law. The courts have uncovered numerous implicit obligations, particularly in mass contracts (for example, an obligation of security, on obligation to provide advice, information or a warning, etc.).

The remedies available for *bilateral/synallagmatic contracts* are based on the notion that in this type of contract, the creditor is also his debtor's debtor.

Either on a temporary basis: the exception of non-performance or non-execution. The creditor suspends the performance--execution of his obligation for as long as his debtor has failed to perform-execute his own. (extrajudicial remedy, new art. 1219 and 1220).

Or permanently: resolution for non-performance releases the creditor entirely from his obligation, the contract being resolved (Civ. Code, new art. 1224 et seq.). The contract may contain a resolutory clause. Failing that, in the case of "sufficiently serious" non--performance, the creditor may ask the court to rescind the contract or he may rescind it unilaterally himself (new art. 1226).

Finally, since the 2016 reform, the creditor is allowed to reduce the price, in the case of imperfect performance of the contract (Civ. Code, new art. 1223).

The debtor cannot be held liable when the non-performance, non-execution, stems from grounds beyond their control; however, the other party to the contract will be released from his own obligation (theory of risks).

The contract is subject to the principle of *immutability*; it may only be revoked or modified by the parties' common consent, or for reasons authorised in law (new art. 1193). Conversely, neither of the parties may modify or breach the contract unilaterally, but there are two exceptions to this principle:

- firstly, the contract can give one or all parties the option to rescind it unilaterally (by means of a rescission clause or right of resiliation); the law itself grants this option in the event of "sufficiently serious" non-performance.
- secondly, the law grants this option in numerous circumstances (for example: the ability to revoke a mandate, real estate leases, etc.) In general terms, the parties are granted

this option in any contract to be executed over an indefinite term.

The principle of immutability raises a problem where there is a change of economic circumstances (unforeseeability) that makes performance-execution excessively onerous for one of the parties (*imprévision*); where the parties are unable to reach an agreement, the judge or arbitrator may adapt the contract (Civ. Code, new art. 1195).

Agreements must be performed in good faith (art. 1134, para. 3; now new art. 1104). This rule governs the behaviour of the parties in the execution of the contract. The contract grants certain prerogatives: i.e. the power to act on the contract solely by one's own decision. Alongside common prerogatives (such as the power to ask for resolution, rescission, invoke a resolutory clause, reject a modification, invoke a particular clause, refuse to approve an assignee or subcontractor, etc.), there are often special prerogatives as well (the power to set a price or option, etc.). In exercising these prerogatives, the parties must act fairly and seek to protect their common interest, where this exists (cooperation contracts).

The sanctions for breaching this obligation range from civil liability for fault to neutralising the exercise of the prerogative (for example, in the case of invoking a resolutory clause of bad faith).

Article 1165 of the Civil Code, now article 1199, lays down the principle of the relative effect of contract: contracts only create obligations between the parties; they cannot cause a detriment to third parties, and can benefit them only in the case of the stipulation for another. However, third parties must respect the legal situation created by the contract (art. 1200).

The *parties* are, first, the persons who have reached a mutual agreement, either personally or through a representative (Civ. Code, new art. 1153 to 1161). The parties' successors (in the case of death, or dissolution of a legal entity) are deemed to continue on the person of the deceased or the dissolved entity; the same applies to the assignee of a contract, in the case of assignment (art. 1216 to

1216-3). On the other hand, the successors under particular title of one party (such as the purchaser of a thing, assignee of a claim or attaching creditor) do not become parties to the contracts entered into by their authors, even in relation to an assigned thing, save exceptions.

Third parties (*penitus extranei*) have no legal relationship with any of the parties. They are not affected by the effects of the contract.

The creditors of either party who are affected by its effects insofar as these effects have a negative effect on their obligor's patrimony (art. 2285).

The contract produces three *effects* with regard to different groups of people.

The contract is a fact, the existence of which must be respected by all. There are two consequences to this. First, a third party who helps one party breach the contract is guilty of an intentional tort/delict (as a third-party accomplice to the breach of contract). Next, where the non-execution of a contract causes damage to a third party, the latter can hold the party in breach liable in tort (as a third-party victim).

The contract can produce other effects than simply creating credit claims and debts, such as: a transfer; the creation of a right in rem; conferring a power of representation; a declaratory effect, etc. These various effects affect everyone—i.e. they are effective against all (opposable). Where the effectiveness of a contract infringes the right of a third party, it may be subject to making a formality of recordation. Moreover, a party's creditors can have an act by their debtor, act that would be prejudicial to their interests, declared unopposable, ineffective, on the basis of the "Paulian" action (Civ. Code, new art. 1341-2).

Contractual obligations are only binding on the parties. This does not prevent a creditor from exercising a right on behalf of a debtor that the latter might fail to exercise, but do so for the benefit of the debtor; this is known as the oblique action ('action oblique') (Civ. Code, new art. 1341-1).

Moreover, a stipulation for the benefit of another (new art. 1205 to 1209) allows a third party to become a creditor without becoming a party: this is the only real exception to the relative effect of contracts.

2. PARTICULAR ASPECTS OF GOVERNMENT CONTRACTS

In administrative law, obligations are derived from the law and unilateral administrative acts. The contract is not examined from the perspective of the theory of obligations but in relation to administrative acts. It is not conceived as a sum of credit claims and debts but as a means of achieving the public-service objectives that govern the actions of public authorities, entities.

The administrative contract complies with the general definition of contract: it is an expression of the wills of two or more parties to reach an agreement, intended to produce legal effects. However, its legal regime is subject to specific characteristics. These are first apparent at the formation stage. The scope of the principle of the autonomy of the will is mitigated by obligations around public disclosure and competitive tendering, which govern the award of numerous administrative contracts and have the effect of limiting the administration's freedom to choose the party with which it wishes to contract. They also appear during performance. Despite the principle of binding force, the administration has various unilateral powers, without their being included in any contractual stipulation (notably, powers to modify and rescind the contract on public-interest grounds) and, in the case of unforeseen events, the other party to the contract has the right to re-establish the balance of the contract in accordance with various legal doctrines (notably *imprévision*). In spite of the principle of the relative effect of contract, the very essence of the administrative contract is that it produces effects in respect of third parties, in accordance with its purpose. A number of contracts thus contain "regulatory clauses" that organise the operation of public services.

CHAPTER TEN

DELICTUAL LIABILITY

In explaining the broad outlines of the law of civil and administrative liability, it is important to recall first that, for an action brought by a victim of harm to be successful, that victim must provide evidence of three things: the harm caused, a tort/delict, and a causal link between the two. Moreover, since the purpose of compensation is to make amends for the harm suffered by the victim, it must be assessed based on the significance of the harm, which underlies the principle of full reparation of harm.

1. LIABILITY UNDER PRIVATE LAW

In order to understand the law of civil or delictual liability, it is important to realise that the tort or delict may be a personal act, or an act by a thing, or an act by another person. In the first case, the perpetrator of the act will be the defendant in the tort or delictual action for liability. In the second, they will be the custodian of the thing. In the third, the action may be brought against the actual perpetrator of the harm and/or against whoever the law or case law has appointed to support the consequences.

To assess the status of positive law, it is important, in the first place, to insist on the fact that, since the Civil Code of 1804, it has moved towards a more objective approach to its rules and notions, and a collective approach to compensation, in favour of the victims.

Until the end of the 19th century, the law of civil/delictual liability set out standards of behaviour intended to prevent harm from occurring and punish the perpetrators of events that cause harm. Conceived as a limit on individual freedom, liability logically rested on the idea of fault. But by the end of the 19th century, the law of delictual liability, which was essentially normative, preventive and repressive, was regarded as inadequate for the risks and dangers of the time. The arrival of mechanisation, increasing urbanisation and the development of science went hand in hand with an increase and worsening of harm. Moreover, the increasing dangerousness of our society prompted a move, in the collective consciousness, towards making compensation for harm, particularly bodily injury, a social imperative, and the objective of securing compensation for victims has taken over from the focus on punishing the unlawful or abnormal behaviour of the perpetrators of harm. Inevitably, the move from a law focused on punishment to one geared more to compensation prompted a decline in the role of fault, since in very many cases of harm, it was difficult for the victim to provide evidence that it had been caused by some form of wrongdoing. As a result, from the end of the 19th century onwards, we saw a proliferation of rules on no-fault liability in both case law and statutes, according to which, not only did the victim not have to demonstrate the wrongdoing committed by the perpetrator of the harm, but the latter was only able to avoid liability by proving that the harm was caused by an event having the characteristics of force majeure.

To illustrate this trend, we can turn first to the identification by the Cour de Cassation of general liability for the acts of things. In order to make things simpler for victims of workplace and traffic accidents, for whom the requirement proving fault frequently resulted in a lack of compensation, the Cour de Cassation created a rule of no-fault liability based on article 1384, para. 1 of the Civil Code, although, in the minds of its drafters, it had no normative authority. Created for the purpose of compensating the victims of workplace accidents (Cass. civ., 16 June 1896, *D.* 1897.1.433), but rendered null and void by the Act of 9 April 1898, the provisions of which governed this category of specific harm, this general liability without fault for the acts of things was recognised a few decades later to allow compensation for the harm suffered by victims of traffic accidents (Ch. réun., 13 February 1930, *Grands arrêts de la jurisprudence civile,* Dalloz, 2015, no. 202). The same phenomenon of objectification also emerges from an analysis of the development of parental liability for the acts of their minor children. Although, for almost two centuries and according to the letter of the Civil Code, the case law/jurisprudence decided that it was an issue of liability for presumed fault, the Cour de Cassation suddenly decided that "only force majeure or fault by the victim could exonerate Mr J. from the liability he automatically incurred for the acts of his minor son, who lived with him" (Cass. 2nd civ. ch., 13 December 1997, *Grands arrêts de la jurisprudence civile,* Dalloz, 2015, no. 217). In other words, parental liability is now a form of no-fault liability; to be released from their liability, parents must now demonstrate that the harm is due to an event having the characteristics of force majeure.

This powerful move towards objectification has also been magnified by modern lawmakers. The Act of 5 July 1985, for example, which attempts to improve the position of victims of road traffic accidents, enables them to receive compensation without having to demonstrate any wrongdoing or fault by the driver or owner of the vehicle involved in the accident. The same applies to the Act of 19 May 1998, which is codified in articles 1386-1 et seq. of the Civil Code, on liability for the acts of defective products. Henceforth, a manufacturer of a defective product that has caused harm is under an absolute obligation of safety as an obligation of result. It can be held liable by the victim on the basis of risk, without the latter being under any obligation to show that the harm was caused by any fault or wrongdoing by the manufacturer.

Alongside the decreasing importance of fault, contemporary law is characterised by a decline in individual responsibility. Various mechanisms to *collectivise and socialise compensation* developed throughout the 20th century, such as liability insurance and guarantee funds, which have fundamentally altered its structure and substance. It is undeniable that these explain, to a very significant extent, the growth in no-fault liability, neutralising a strict approach to the person responsible. Indeed, judges have increasingly fewer scruples about reaching a decision of no-fault liability in respect of the perpetrator if they know that the latter will not personally bear the financial burden of paying compensation, which will ultimately fall on insurance policyholders as a whole, or be a matter of national solidarity.

Even more striking is the gradual removal of the whole idea of liability, with the increasing socialisation of compensation payments. Indeed, the guarantee funds set up by the legislature are an expression of the imperative of national solidarity and do not require the victim who calls on them to establish any kind of liability to be compensated for the harm they have suffered.

2. ADMINISTRATIVE LIABILITY

The *Blanco* decision (TC, 8 Feb. 1876, *GAJA*, p. 1) established, on the one hand, the independence of administrative liability in relation to the law of delictual or civil liability and, on the other, the exclusive jurisdiction of the administrative courts to rule on disputes falling within this area of this special form of liability. In a nutshell, public authorities are governed by administrative liability, while private individuals and entities are subject to civil/delictual liability rules. Moreover, a liability action brought by a victim against a public authority must be heard by a judge in the administrative courts, while any action they may bring against a private individual or entity must be heard in the ordinary courts.

Explaining the substance of the law on administrative liability means examining first, the rules on jurisdiction and secondly, the substantive rules that govern it.

With regard to the rules on jurisdiction, since the *Blanco* decision, the administrative courts have exclusive jurisdiction to rule on disputes relating to administrative liability. They therefore cannot be heard in the ordinary courts. However, to draw the line between the jurisdiction of the administrative and ordinary courts means not focusing on the status of the person carrying out the activity that has caused the harm, but on "the legal nature of the activity involved" (Ph. Brun, *Responsabilité civile extracontractuelle,* Litec, 2014, no. 34). It follows therefore that, even if a public authority is the source of the harm suffered by a private individual or entity, jurisdiction may sometimes be assigned to the ordinary rather than the administrative courts. This is the case with the liability of industrial and commercial public services. Jurisdiction is also assigned to the ordinary courts when the harm has been caused by the personal wrongdoing or fault of an employee of a public authority, which can be separated out from their official function, while it must be assigned to the administrative courts when the employee causes harm following a simple administrative fault of service during the performance of their duties, for which the administration is solely liable.

As regards the substantive rules, the liability of the public authority is the result of a compromise between two imperatives of legal policy: protecting the interests of the administration by avoiding situations where it can be too easily held liable in carrying out its duties, and protecting the interests of victims.

The ordinary law in administrative matters is fault-based liability. The existence of an administrative fault, *faute de service*, depends on the judge's view of various concrete elements: "He must ask himself what someone was legitimately entitled to expect from the service, given the degree of difficulty of the task at hand, the circumstances, the staff and physical resources available, etc." (Ch. Guettier, *Droit de la responsabilité et des contrats,* Ph. le Tourneau (ed.), Dalloz, 2014, no. 409). It is manifested in various ways: either it is based on an unlawful action, which is attributable to the public authority; or it results from the ineffective operation or defective organisation of the public service. In some cases, the administration's liability is based on a presumption of fault, for example, for harm caused by some public infrastructure to users, or in relation to hospital liability. In certain other cases, particularly in relation to sovereign powers exercised by the public authority, the administration can only be held liable if the victim establishes the existence of gross fault or misconduct. Initially, this requirement was used to temper the Conseil d'Etat's position, which, in the *Blanco* decision, asserted that the liability of the public authority was "neither general nor absolute." Initially, this concept was used by the courts to reduce the number of cases of non-liability of the administration, in statutes or contracts. Subsequently, the administrative courts have, on the contrary, used it to reduce the scope of liability of the public authorities, when the general principle of their responsibility was recognized (Ch. Guettier, *op. and loc. cit.*, spec. no. 430).

As with civil or delictual liability, and for identical reasons, a system of objective liability currently coexists—and has done since the end of the 19th century—with a system of subjective liability. As a result, a public authority can be held liable without the victim having to prove any kind of fault, and can only be exonerated by establishing that the harm was caused by an external, unforeseeable event beyond its control. A system of this kind benefits the users of public hospital services in the event of medical accidents, people who are occasionally employed by the administration and third-party victims of harm caused by public works (for a detailed analysis, see Ch. Guettier, *op. and loc. cit.*, no. 458 et seq.).

CHAPTER ELEVEN

QUASI-CONTRACTS

Quasi-contracts are the result of a historical misunderstanding, probably attributable to a questionable reading of Roman law by the glossators (F. Zenati-Castaing and Th. Revet, *Cours de droit civil, Contrats, Théorie générale—Quasi-contrats*, Puf, 2014, no. 225), and since 1804, at least, have been viewed as a separate source of obligation. They have been covered since the ordonnance n° 2016-131 of 10 February 2016, reforming the law of contracts, the general regime of obligations and proof of obligations, by sub-title III ("Other sources of obligations") of title III ("Sources of obligations") of the Civil Code. They are defined as "purely voluntary acts that result in an obligation of the person who benefits from them without having any right to that benefit and sometimes an obligation to the author of the act to another person" (art. 1300), it being specified that this sub-title governs "the quasi-contracts of the management of the affairs of another, the payment of a thing not due, and unjustified enrichment." It is stated in the report to the President of the Republic on the 2016 ordonnance, that the definition chosen "is sufficiently flexible to allow the judge, if necessary, to recognise behaviours that should place their instigators under an obligation to pay compensation, in spite of the silence of the law" and that "the non-exhaustive list of quasi-contracts in the second paragraph implies that there may be unnamed quasi-contracts, whose legal regime is not provided for in the Civil Code". There are therefore unnamed quasi-contracts alongside named ones.

MANAGEMENT OF ANOTHER'S AFFAIRS ('gestion d'affaires') is the first quasi-contract named in the Civil Code. It refers to the management by an individual of "the affairs of another person," the principal, in order to render him a service. For example, an individual repairs the roof of his neighbour's house while the latter is on holiday before a storm comes, or an individual pays another person's debts to avoid having his property being seized. In order for a situation to be classified as management of another's affairs, the action must be spontaneous (the person who has taken action was not obliged to do so), altruistic (the person who has taken action knowingly acted for someone else, regardless of whether it was in her own interest also) and useful (the action was beneficial), whether the principal was aware of it or not; if the principal was aware, he neither agreed nor disagreed (if he agreed, there would be a contract rather than a quasi-contract). The management may consist in carrying out material acts or entering into legal transactions. The gestor-manager is subject to "all the obligations which he would have owed as a mandatary" (even if he was not solely involved in legal transactions—far from it); specifically, he is required to act as a "reasonable person" (the judge can, depending on the circumstances, and as an exception to the principle of full compensation, moderate the compensation due to the principal because of mistakes by the intervenor), and "carry on with the management" until the principal or his successor is able to take over. For his part, the principal must, on the one hand, "fulfil the commitments contracted by the manager in his interest" and on the other hand, reimburse the latter for the expenses incurred in his interest (which carry interest from the day they are paid)—but does not (and this is an essential point) owe the manager any remuneration—and compensate him for any harm suffered as a result of his action. Should the manager find a personal interest in his management, the costs of the commitments made, expenses incurred and damages would be split in proportion to each party's interest in the common affair. Before the reform, the principal's ratification of the management prevented him from contesting that the conditions for management of another's affairs had been met; since the reform, it has been viewed as a "mandate", which raises certain questions. In any event, in the absence of ratification and if the conditions for management of another's affairs are not met, but the principal has still benefited from the management undertaken, he is obliged to compensate the manager in accordance to the rules on unjustified enrichment, which implies that the conditions for this quasi-contract are met, whereas those for the management of another's affairs are not: this could be the case if someone had believed—wrongly—that he was obliged to act in the interest of another person when this was not actually the case (if he simply believed, wrongly, that he was acting freely in his own interest, but in reality was acting in the interest of another person, he could be considered to have acted with a view to making a "personal profit," which would prevent a finding of unjustified enrichment, although this is debatable).

PAYMENT OF A THING NOT DUE ('paiement de l'indu') is the second quasi-contract named. The principle is that "every payment presupposes a debt" and that "what has been received without being due is subject to restitution", on the understanding, however, that voluntary payment for a natural obligation does not give rise to restitution and that restitution may be reduced if the payment is based on a fault.

It should be noted, by way of preliminary observation, that although the law does not treat, as a *payment not due, a payment that has become undue* following retroactive cancellation (nullity, rescission, etc.) of a debt, nonetheless, restitution is governed by the relevant rules set out in articles 1352 et seq. of the Civil Code. This being said, the regime of a payment not due, and in particular, the action for restitution arising from it, differ according to whether the *accipiens* was a creditor or not. The fundamental distinction over whether the *accipiens* was a creditor or not can be justified in arbitrating between the interests at stake, namely the interest of the *accipiens* in retaining what he has received and the interest of the *solvens* in getting back what he has paid out. In fact, the interest of the *accipiens* in retaining what he has been paid, when he was owed nothing, is still unlawful and it is difficult to see why an action for restitution should be subject to special conditions. Conversely, the interest of the *accipiens* in retaining what he has been paid, when it was owed to him, is legitimate, so much so that in this case, there are two opposing but legitimate interests: the interest of the *solvens* in obtaining restitution of what he paid out, when he was under no obligation to do so, and that of the *accipiens* in retaining what he received and was owed him, particularly since payment on behalf of another is perfectly valid. The one explains the other. Thus, an *accipiens who is not a creditor* is required to restore solely on the basis of the payment he received (unless, of course, even though the law does not make it explicit, the *solvens* intended it as a gift). In the specific case where the *solvens* would not have actually paid the right creditor—whom he will have to pay in any case and, having made a mistake, had to pay twice—the question has arisen of whether, in order to simplify the process, the real creditor could take direct action against the *accipiens* on the basis of payment not due, to avoid increasing the number of actions (by the *solvens* against the *accipiens*, and the real creditor against the *solvens*). The case law prior to the reform, however, was opposed to allowing "direct action" of this kind on the basis of payment not due, although such an action on the basis of unjustified enrichment seems conceivable. The 2006 ordonnance does not contain any provisions in this respect. Conversely, *if the accipiens was a creditor*, and the *solvens* paid another person's debt, the action for restitution can only be exercised by the *solvens* against the *accipiens* on the condition, in this case, that it can be proven that the payment was made in error (for example, someone's erroneous belief that he was an heir causing him to pay off the debts of the estate) or under duress, given that in any case, the action will not be available if the *accipiens* has destroyed his title or abandoned the securities guaranteeing the debt, because of difficulties in recovering the sums owed to him. Again, it has been asked whether, to simplify the process, the *solvens* could not take action directly against the real debtor on the basis of payment not due, to avoid increasing the number of actions (by the *solvens* against the *accipiens* and the *accipiens* against the debtor). The case law prior to the reform accepted such an action, generally on the basis of unjustified enrichment. In this case, the 2006 ordonnance is sensitive to a direct action and offers the *solvens* the possibility of taking action against the debtor but, again, provided he proves that he made his payment to the *accipiens* in error.

UNJUSTIFIED ENRICHMENT is the third named quasi-contract, following the recognition by the 2006 ordonnance of this judge-made quasi-contract, created by a decision of the Cour de Cassation of 15 June 1892. Its benefit is to correct anyone's unjustified enrichment to the detriment of another person, other than through management of another's affairs or payment not due. For example, an individual has worked in his cohabitee's business without payment or a property owner has benefited from the works carried out by a contractor who has not been paid by the tenant. As the Civil Code now states (Civ. C. art. 1303), "a person who benefits from an unjustified enrichment to the detriment of another person owes to the person who is impoverished as a result an indemnity amounting to the lesser of the two values of the enrichment and the impoverishment"; however, the impoverished party will be entitled to compensation equal to the higher of these two values when the enriched party acted in bad faith and the compensation paid to the impoverished party can still be moderated by the judge if the impoverishment is the result of its own wrongdoing. In any event, the impoverished party can only invoke this quasi-contract when the enrichment is not justified by the fulfilment of an obligation (contractual or legal) by the impoverished party, his intention to make a gift or an act carried out with a view to personal profit (which is where it differs from management of another's affairs). Unjustified enrichment is a secondary mechanism, insofar as the impoverished party can rely on it only if no other action is available to him or he is confronted with a legal obstacle, such as prescription. In this respect, it is important to distinguish between two scenarios. *Where no other action is available to the claimant*, he ought to be able to act without difficulty on the basis of unjustified enrichment. However, the case law is hesitant where the claimant bases his primary action on a contract of which he intends to furnish proof and is only invoking the quasi-contract on a subsidiary basis, any time the judge believes that proof of the alleged contract has not been provided. *Where another action is available to the claimant*, but he is prevented from pursuing it by a legal obstacle, such as prescription, the action on the quasi-contract will not be heard, but for reasons that relate more to the fact that the enrichment is justified (by law) than the requirement of subsidiarity.

With regard to unnamed quasi-contracts, it is questionable whether, following the 2016 ordonnance, the "lottery quasi-contract", which is based on the deceptive announcement of a promised win, will prosper any further. The Cour de Cassation has used this to order mail-order companies to pay recipients the winnings promised deceptively in misleading letters, small print that, in reality, they had been selected only towards drawing lots. The case law has been keen to order lottery organisers to deliver on misleadingly promised winnings to dissuade them from acting in this way, and to compensate their victims. It has not been able to find both a legitimate and appropriate source among the traditional sources of obligations. Extracontractual or delictual liability was a legitimate foundation insofar as it fulfilled the conditions, but inappropriate insofar as it did not allow the winnings to be awarded, as the harm suffered was negligible. Conversely, the juridical act appeared to be an appropriate foundation insofar as it allowed the award of the winnings, but unlawful, since it was devoid of intent to be bound on the part of the company. Faced with this dilemma, on 6 September 2002, the Cour de Cassation opted for the quasi-contract: "the organiser of a lottery who announces a win to a named person without pointing out the existence of a random element, is obliged, by this purely voluntary act, to deliver it" (*Bull. civ.*, no. 6), provided the person acted in good faith (*Bull. civ.*, no.

5). This distorted the nature of the quasi-contract: not only was it fault-based, but there was a lack of unjust enrichment. However, resorting to quasi-contract could be justified by the ambiguous wording of former article 1371 of the Civil Code: "Quasi-contracts are purely voluntary acts of man, from which there results some undertaking towards a third party, and sometimes a reciprocal undertaking of both parties." It seems much more problematic in light of the new definition: "Quasi-contracts are purely voluntary acts that result in an obligation of the person who benefits from them without having any right to that benefit, and sometimes an obligation of the author of the act to another person." (Civ. Code, art. 1300, cited above).

CHAPTER TWELVE

BUSINESS ENTITIES

The freedom to form a business entity is constitutionally enshrined (art. 4 of the Declaration of the Rights of Man of 1789). It was also recognised in the form of freedom of trade and industry by the Allarde decree of 1791. It is the freedom to exercise an economic activity in accordance with the regulations in effect, on the understanding that the latter should not be disproportionate to the objective pursued.

1. FORM OF BUSINESS ENTITIES

1.1. SOLE TRADER

Almost two thirds of business owners choose to operate as sole traders: setting up as a sole trader simply involves registering a commercial activity with the Trade and Companies Register or an artisanal activity with the Répertoire des métiers and making a declaration to the social security authorities (Urssaf).

If turnover remains below certain thresholds (€82,200 for a commercial activity involving sales or accommodation and €32,900 for a service provider or independent professional), the owner of a so-called *micro-business* can take advantage of a simplified regime for accounting, social security and tax matters.

A one-person business has no separate legal personality, which means that the business owner is free to manage it at his discretion but is subject to unlimited liability, with the notable exception of their main residence, which business creditors have been unable to seize since the Macron legislation of 6 August 2015. Waiving the right to freedom from seizability is, however, possible: it is frequently sought by banks faced with this immunity from liability in relation to land ownership.

Since a statute of 15 June 2010, however, a sole trader has been able to operate as a *sole trader with limited liability* ('entrepreneur individuel à responsabilité limitée'—EIRL). Trading as an EIRL involves creating a designated set of protected business assets that are accounted for separately, allocated in accordance with a declaration made by the sole trader. Any right of pursuit by the business's creditors is therefore limited to the designated assets only, excluding the owner's personal assets.

However, the EIRL has been less successful than the authorities had hoped, undoubtedly because it is a complex mechanism that does not protect the business owner from unlimited liability on all his assets in cases of fraud or a serious breach of the asset allocation or accounting rules.

1.2. TRADING AS A COMPANY/ CORPORATION/"SOCIÉTÉ"

Involving elements of both partnerships (in which shares can be transferred by agreement, *intuitu personae*) and companies/ corporations (where liability is limited to the amount paid in by the shareholders), the private limited company (*'société à responsabilité limitée'*—SARL) alone represents over half of all company structures: it is particularly popular with small and medium-sized enterprises (SMEs). It may have a single shareholder as an 'entreprise unipersonnelle à responsabilité limitée' (EURL) or up to 100, and can be formed with share capital of one euro. The company is managed by a natural person.

Almost 40% of companies are formed as *non-trading partnerships* ('sociétés civiles'). Almost three quarters of them are immovable property companies ('sociétés civiles immobilières'—SCI); they are also found in the professional and agricultural sectors. The fact that they are non-trading and the partners' unlimited joint liability distinguishes them from commercial partnerships ('sociétés en nom collectif'—SNC) in which all the partners trade and are solidarily liable for an unlimited amount (less than 2% of companies). There is no minimum capital requirement for partnerships, which are free and formed *intuitu personae*. Since decisions must be taken unanimously, they cannot be formed be a single person.

The number of *'sociétés par actions simplifiées'* (SAS) has now exceeded the number of limited companies ('sociétés anonymes'—SA) with either a board of directors or an executive board and supervisory board, multiple shareholders and a still distinctive institutional character; in practice, SAs now tend to be reserved for companies whose shares are publicly traded. The SAS was introduced in 1994 and now represent almost 5% of registered companies. They owe their success to the extensive freedom and limited liability granted to shareholders: unlike the SA, which has a minimum capital requirement of €37,000, an SAS can be formed with share capital of one euro and can have a single shareholder ('société par actions simplifiée unipersonnelle'—SASU). They are led by a chair/president, with other company bodies created in accordance with the articles of association.

A company can also be formed as a limited partnership ('commandite simple') or partnership limited by shares ('commandite par actions'); the managing partners ('commandités') are solidarily bound, unlike the other partners ('commanditaires'), whose liability is limited.

Finally, several companies can act together by forming an economic interest group ('groupement d'intérêt économique'—GIE), whose activities must be auxiliary to those of its members.

2. DIFFICULTIES ENCOUNTERED BY BUSINESS ENTERPRISES

French law deals with business entities in difficulty either through insolvency proceedings or by offering an alternative.

Where there is a chance that the business may be able to recover, it is possible to address its difficulties, whatever they may be, using alternative methods in a confidential environment before the situation deteriorates further, which is more effective and less disruptive to the economic environment. Even a business that has become insolvent, provided it has only occurred within less than 45 days, can make use of either an *ad hoc* mandate or conciliation and ask a judge to appoint a judicial mandatary/administrator to negotiate an agreement between the debtor and their creditors, with the aim of overcoming its difficulties. Since the *ad hoc* mandatary/administrator or conciliator has no authority to force the creditors to negotiate, these mechanisms are considered as amicable procedures. All the administrator or conciliator can do is persuade them, by pointing to how their situation would be worse if the negotiation failed and was replaced by insolvency proceedings. Another characteristic of these procedures is speed: an agreement must be secured within a few months (specifically limited to five in the case of conciliation).

It is also possible to avoid insolvency proceedings since the ordonnance of 12 March 2014, by allowing a natural person debtor to use a procedure called "professional re-establishment" ('rétablissement professionnel'), which results in all the debts that have been declared as being wiped out in a very short period of time (four months). The procedure is opened by the court, which appoints a judicial mandatary/administrator to check, under the authority of a single judge, that the debtor meets the eligibility criteria, i.e. if he has assets of less than €5,000, has no employees and has not committed any wrongdoing or fraud that would justify actions being taken against him which, since they could only be taken in the context of winding-up ordered by the court, would deprive the debtor of the possibility of professional re-establishment.

If the business's difficulties are too severe for them to be dealt with by an amicable procedure, the debtor will apply for insolvency proceedings to be opened. If he is insolvent, i.e. his available (liquid) assets are not sufficient to cover his short-term liabilities, this is not an option but an obligation. He must then apply to the court to enter receivership (if there is a prospect of recovery for the business) or be wound up if there is no chance of it continuing; if he does not do so, he risks being barred from managing a company. If payments are not suspended, he may be entitled to apply for a safeguarding procedure, which (like receivership) involves adopting a reorganisation plan. Safeguarding exists in two simplified forms: accelerated safeguarding and accelerated financial safeguarding, which have been recently introduced into our code to allow the adoption of a *prepack* plan, i.e., a restructuring solution accepted by a majority of the creditors in an amicable procedure and then imposed on the minority shareholders by voting in creditors' committees, which are convened for this purpose.

Both receivership and safeguarding aim to restructure the business and agree on a plan to settle its liabilities, either negotiated with creditors or imposed by the court. If the creditors accept the debtor's proposals, either individually or in a vote, by a two-thirds majority in the creditors' committees, which must be convened above certain thresholds (150 employees or 20 million in turnover), they will be paid subject to delays, reductions in the debts or even by converting their claims into shares. If they refuse, all the court can do is impose payment terms of no more than 10 years.

Finally, judicial receivership is designed to liquidate all the debtor's assets and distribute the proceeds between his creditors. However, this final aim can be frustrated if the business is sold as a whole under an assignment plan ordered by the court. In this case, the creditors are sacrificed since they will only be entitled to the price—often modest, and out of their control—paid by the buyer and bear the cancellation of the securities placed on the debtor's property, with the notable exception of those conferring a right of retention and of the fiduciary security without dispossession.

3. FRAMEWORK OF BUSINESS ACTIVITIES

Some part of consumer law is derived from the transposition of European minimum and maximum harmonisation directives. These demonstrate how consumer law has become market law: states cannot give consumers greater protection, in order to avoid distorting competition between operators in different Member States.

French law defines the consumer as "any natural person acting for reasons outside the scope of their commercial, industrial, artisanal or professional activities" but in some cases, the definition is extended to the protection of "non-professional" legal entities.

French law offers a high level of consumer protection, notably thanks to the various actions brought by consumer associations (including class actions) and the role of judges.

However, this level of protection had to be reduced to ensure compliance with Directive 2005/29. Henceforth, the former bans *per se* on sales with bonuses, paid lotteries and tied selling, are dependent on proving that a promotional transaction is unfair.

Competition law is primarily driven by protection of the weaker party and a requirement of fairness.

Unfair B2B (business-to-business) practices, which are not defined in law, are those that depart from good commercial practices.

The law lists a large number of them, but most disputes centre on two of them: the ban on a significant imbalance (Comm. Code., art. L. 442-6, I, 2.) and the sudden termination of an established commercial relationship (art. L. 442-6, I, 5.).

The effectiveness of this legislation relies on the existence of specialist judges, and independent action to protect the market by the Minister of the Economy. The latter may demand a civil fine (an increasingly common mechanism), have a contract declared null and void or seek restitution, which will deprive the perpetrator of their anticipated unlawful profits. It is generally, but not exclusively, used against mass distribution.

The requirement for fair competition is based on article 1382 of the Civil Code. There are four hypotheses: confusion, denigration, internal disorganisation in the business and general disorganisation of the market.

The adaptability of this theory is demonstrated by the emergence of parasitic competition and the fact that action for unfair competition is increasingly based on the competitor's failure to respect consumer law.

In terms of protecting the market in the strict sense of the term, French law is very close to European Union law. It applies to business entities, defined as economic units with the ability to behave autonomously in the market.

Are prohibited agreements to restrain trade (Comm. Code, art. L. 420-1), which presuppose a common intention to distort competition, or have the effect of doing so. They can be justified by economic progress or some form of legislation. Large cartels are the most harmful of these agreements. Conversely, vertical restrictions on competition are considered less serious and will often be exempted.

Abuse of market dominance is also prohibited (Comm. Code, art. L. 420-2, para. 1). Individual or collective market dominance lies in the ability to hinder effective competition in the relevant market. There are two forms of abuse: elimination or abuse of dominant position. Previously, the prohibited practices of the dominant business were prohibited *per se*. The analysis of abuse is now much more concrete, taking into account any gains in terms of efficiency, but it is also less predictable.

There are other prohibitions in French law, such as the abuse of economic dependence and abusively low prices, but they have not been as successful as hoped.

In practical terms, the law on anti-competitive practices is implemented by the Autorité de la concurrence, the French competition commission, which is an independent administrative authority, though subject to article 6 of the European Convention on Human Rights, insofar as it inflicts punitive sanctions, which can be as high as 10% of the group's consolidated turnover.

Businesses may propose some commitments or transactions in order to avoid sanction. A leniency procedure will be offered to a member of a cartel that reports it, as part of efforts to uncover them.

Since 2008, the Competition Commission has also been responsible for examining market concentration, which was previously a political matter. The minister has retained only a right of veto, for non competition-related reasons, although it has never used it.

Concentration implies a change in the control of a business entity (Comm. Code, art. L. 430-1). The Competition Commission focuses on market concentrations above a certain threshold, but do not have a European scale. Businesses often have to make some commitments to secure an authorisation.

CHAPTER THIRTEEN

LABOR AND EMPLOYMENT LAW

Labour law is based on the premise that an individual (the employee) makes a contractual commitment to work for the benefit of another person (the employer), in accordance with the employer's instructions, if applicable with tools provided by them, and in return for compensation.

However, not all working relationships are covered by labour law: there is still a body of law for the public service, which consists on the one hand, of a common core, notably recruitment by competitive examination and a guaranteed income for life, and on the other, a vast set of special rules for each occupation and ministry. Employees of local authorities and staff working in public hospitals have been given a status similar to that of public service employees. There is even *ad hoc* labour law for staff who are considered non "post holders" (non-titulaires) of public-sector functions.

It is also important to note that if the employment contract is governed by labour law, it also triggers the application of:

- social security law, and in particular, the rules of the general social security system, which provides partial coverage for loss of income in cases of inability to work, disability or old age, and covers certain health costs and family expenses;

- unemployment insurance law, in the case of involuntary loss of employment, which will provide a replacement income on a temporary basis;
- the law on compulsory top-up welfare protection (top-up pension schemes, top-up group insurance for health care costs, continued payment of salary if the employee is unable to work, life insurance for executives or compulsory top-up welfare protection resulting from collective bargaining agreements);
- even, on an optional basis, additional pension benefits (so-called "pension funds") or additional personal risk insurance, which can also translate into obligations to fund these plans, through premiums and contributions that may be partially or fully levied from the employee's pay;
- specific tax law, designed to encourage certain forms of welfare protection through partial tax reliefs.

French doctrine sometimes use the term "social law" to cover labour law and welfare legislation as a whole.

The original Civil Code devoted just two articles to "hiring of services", one noting the abolition of serfdom and the other that "the master's assertion on the share of wages shall be believed".

Labour law has developed from these summary rules:

- it was originally, and is still, an expression of the employer's power to direct their employees and is manifested in regulations and collective standards of discipline, combined with sanctions. The fundamental distinction, even today, between executives and non-executives stems from the power to organise the business;
- later, it was and still is, a national law on the protection of health and safety, and therefore of the persons of dependent workers. It is common to trace the origins of French

labour law back to the laws limiting the working hours of children in the middle of the 19th century. Since then, compulsory standards that can be monitored by public officials and may involve criminal sanctions have increased. This national law is not identical for all businesses: its application depends on the size of the workforce;
- it is also the result of established practices and of the power relationship between the employer or employers and a group of employees or a trade union; agreements to end disputes gradually becoming collective bargaining agreements, tools which were recognised by the national legal system, first in 1918, and later in 1936, along with employee representation.

As a consequence, labour law:

- is necessarily multidimensional: while it provides a degree of protection for the person who is considered the weaker party in an employment contract, it also serves to stabilise and harmonise working conditions and therefore, the cost of labour as a factor in the business or type of.
- must necessarily adapt to new ways of working: examples here include the increasing autonomy some employees want, which makes certain concepts outdated or difficult to apply as, for example, the work rate, or working hours more generally, or the development of information and communications technologies, which potentially make some of the central concepts of labour law obsolete, such as the notion of a workplace, the distinction between dependent and independent, basic concepts of labor law;
- has been built up in successive strata, resulting in legislative inflation: the French Labour Code, for example, has over 8,000 articles, and there are over 1,300 sector agreements, plus countless company-wide agreements.

- draws ultimately, at least in part, on European Union law, which, with its jurisdiction in areas such as workplace health and safety, gender equality and support for migration, and because of the liberalisation of cross-border service prestations, is tending to harmonise working conditions across Member States;
- is underpinned by fundamental rights, notably through the decisions of the European Court of Human Rights or the decisions of the Constitutional Council on priority questions on constitutionality [question prioritaire de constitutionalité].

1. INDIVIDUAL RELATIONSHIPS

Labor Law has numerous specific characteristics.

The characteristic exchange of subordinate labour for salary found in the employment contract obliges the employer to provide the agreed work and to pay the salary. The pre-contractual phase and the execution of an employment contract of unlimited duration are characterised by key principles, such as non-discrimination on grounds of gender, age, sexual orientation, state of health, etc. In addition, the autonomy of will of the parties to the agreement is strictly governed by suppletive rules of law, possibly supplemented or amended by collective bargaining agreements: a statutory minimum wage, maximum daily, weekly and monthly working hours, the right to a daily and weekly rest period and compulsory paid leave, plus the law on working conditions and health and safety, and the rules on compulsory contributions to welfare protection schemes (notably, the general social security system and compulsory top-up welfare protection schemes), which shape the working relationship.

The peculiarity of the unlimited duration employment contract lies in the rules governing unilateral termination by the employer (dismissal). Unlike resignation, which is only limited by misuse, an employee can only be dismissed for a real and serious reason, which may be a disciplinary matter (in which case, it is the most radical sanction for the employee's breach of an established rule), non-disciplinary (if the employee is unsuited to the job, lacks professional capability, etc.) or an economic issue ("removal or transformation of the job, or modification of an essential element of the employment contract, notably in response to economic difficulties or technological changes" L.1233-3 of the Labour Code.)

Dismissal requires compliance with a particular procedure, which still includes a written notification of the grounds for dismissal, preceded by an interview between the employee and employer, except in the case of large-scale redundancies.

Termination by mutual agreement can only take place subject to approval (or authorisation for so-called "protected" employees) by the labour administration, except where the Labour Code itself provides otherwise.

The term "precarious" contracts, which points to the contract of unlimited duration as the ordinary and common contract, covers fixed-term employment contracts and employment contracts performed in a business that is not the employer, under a hiring of services agreement, known as "temporary" or "interim" work. This category also includes the part-time employment contract, which may be unlimited in time or with a fixed-term.

There are limited grounds for using fixed-term or temporary employment contracts; they must be written—in a precisely regulated way—failing which, they can be reclassified as of unlimited duration. In addition, there is an established principle of equal treatment in relation to employees with unlimited duration employment contract.

The fixed-term and temporary employment contract cannot, in principle, end before their agreed term unless the parties agree otherwise, or in the case of serious misconduct (faute grave), force majeure or inability, or to allow the employee to take up a job of unlimited duration.

2. COLLECTIVE BARGAININGS

Collective labour law is characterised by a multiplicity of employee representatives and its autonomous normative power, which is both stimulated and governed by legislative and regulatory powers. It is accompanied by a very special form of highly developed criminal law.

The three statutory staff representation bodies, which appeared at key dates in French social history (staff representatives—1936; works councils—1945; health, safety and working conditions committee—1982) were succeeded in 2017 by a single, elected staff representation body, the economic and social committee (CSE), chaired by the employer, with both elected members and (if applicable) trade-union representatives. The body's main functions are to manage a budget for social and cultural activities, and to express the views of employees. The employer is under an obligation to inform and consult the CSE, notably when decisions are being taken on the management and economic and financial development of the business, or if there are changes to the way work is organised. Terms of office last for four years, unless a shorter period is agreed.

Employee trade unions are *ad hoc* legal entities, whose purpose is to "defend the material and personal interests of employees".

Freedom to join a trade union is a universally recognised and protected human right. It is also characterised as a principle that is "especially necessary to our times" by the Preamble to the 1946 Constitution.

An important distinction is drawn, however, between unions that are representative and those that are not: the former have the power to enter into a collective labour convention or agreement, appoint one or more trade union representatives or draw up lists of candidates for the first round of staff representative elections. This system of representation is primarily the result of periodic measures, starting with voting in professional elections in each business entity, votes which are then consolidated at the sector level and then the national level by the labour administration.

The representativeness of employers' organisations is calculated based on the number of businesses that belong to them. The first measurement of support by the labour administration was carried out in 2017 and will be repeated every four years.

French collective labour law is characterised by numerous legislative and regulatory incentives to negotiate, to such an extent that, since 1 January 2016, the 17 existing obligations to negotiate have been grouped into three extensive business negotiations:

- two annual negotiations on compensation, working hours, sharing the added value on the one hand, and on the quality of life at work, on the other;
- a three-yearly negotiation on jobs and professional careers, that can also cover the generational contract (a measure aimed at replacing older workers with younger ones).

Another characteristic of French collective labour law is the number of national interprofessional agreements, signed at the instigation of the government and often "transposed" more or less fully into regulatory or legislative provisions (an example would be the national interprofessional agreement of January 2013, which was transposed into the Security of Employment Act of June 2013), which set the pace for the creation of labour law.

Finally, social partners have, in addition to setting uniform working conditions for periods of varying length, depending on the sector, created additional welfare protection schemes and even joint management institutions and *ad hoc* not-for-profit insurance organisations.

Strikes, i.e. the collective and concerted cessation of work to push through certain claims by employees, are both a power relationship and a means of exerting collective pressure by a group of workers seeking justice for itself but above all, a right viewed as one of the "necessary principles of our times", but which must be exercised in accordance with paragraph 7 of the Preamble of the 1946 Constitution, "within the framework of the laws governing it". One of the notable characteristics of French law is that it views the right to strike as an employee's individual right, which is exercised collectively. As a consequence, a strike does not have to be led or endorsed by a trade union to be lawful. Nonetheless, it must be manifested by a clear cessation of work by several employees (therefore, at least two), so that the resulting suspension of the employment contract is not reclassified as defective performance. Strikes are subject to stricter rules (such as giving advance notice of a strike) in certain sectors, such as air and rail transport, because of their potentially harmful consequences for third parties.

Striking is prohibited for certain categories of public servants such as the military, and governed by the law on the public service: the strike must be endorsed by a trade union, which must notify its intention to ask employees to stop work.

A *lock-out* is the temporary closure of a business decided by the employer in response to a strike: non-striking employees who are "locked out" are no longer paid. This type of pressure by the employer is prohibited in French law, except on essential security grounds.